Broadcasting: New Patron of Hindustani Music

BROADCASTING:
New Patron of Hindustani Music

B.N. GOSWAMI

1996
Sharada Publishing House
DELHI - 110035

First Published 1996

ISBN : 81-85616-36-1

Published by
B.L. BANSAL
for SHARADA PUBLISHING HOUSE
(Publishers on India's Past and Present)
40, Anand Nagar, Inderlok,
DELHI - 110035 Ph. 511 6763, 511 7390

Laser Typeset
IDEAL PRINTERS, Delhi - 110007

Printed at
SANTOSH OFFSET, Delhi - 110035.

In the memory of
my departed 'Dada'
Shri Rampal Goswami

Contents

Preface

The word 'Broadcast' was very much in the dictionary prior to the invention of radio or wireless telegraphy, but its meaning was 'to scatter seeds, etc. over a wide surface'. However, after the invention of radio the meaning of the word 'broadcast' changed 'to disseminate audiable matter from a wireless transmitter'. In fact, the word 'broadcast' got its real meaning after the radio became a social institution. In the shortest period of time, radio became the cheapest and the best source of disseminating information as compared to the other media of communication, and its impact on the society was quick and instant.

Being in AIR for over 18 years in programming, I have had the idea to conduct a study as regards the impact of broadcasting on Hindustani Classical Music. I have also benefitted greatly by interviews, conversations and interactions during my day to day working.

There is lot of published material available on broadcasting and its impact on the society, I tried to include each and every information available, including interviews. However, much have been left due to non-availability of information after so many efforts. Whatever was available, has been consolidated, studied, analysed and concluded in this study.

I am grateful to my friends, in and outside the organisation, without the help of them, it was impossible to complete the work. I would like to mention the name of Shri G.S. Arya, Station Director, who extended all possible help to complete this work. It will also be appropriate to mention the name of late Shri S.K. Johar, a senior programme officer (associated with AIR since 1956), who, by virtue of his experience in the organisation, not only given me valuable advice, but also checked the manuscript. I must express my great regards to him.

I cannot forget the hearty co-operation of my wife Smt. Bimala Goswami and my kids (Arvind, Abha & Anuradha) who kept me away from household resposibilities during the process of my research.

Laborious work of final proof reading was completed by Sh. K. N. Goswami (my younger brother) who deserve my thanks.

In the last, I am sure that this work has been completed with the blessings of my Pujya Guruji, Dr. Asit Kumar Banerjee.

26.1.1995 **B.N. GOSWAMI**

1

Introduction

> "A tribal and feudal hierarchy of traditional kind collapses quickly when it meets any hot medium of the mechanical, uniform and repetitive kind."
>
> Marshall Mcluhan

One remarkable fact, which emerges from the study of history of mankind, is that every new invention and extension of men brought revolutionary changes in the social, cultural and political structures of the society. However, the intensity of the revolution depend on the quality of invention. The invention of wheel, several thousand years before, must have changed the way of life of the mankind, and taming of horse and bullocks were the counter revolutions in this chain. For next several thousand years nothing more happened until the invention of steam engine, which was responsible for the industrial revolution in the Europe in nineteenth century.

Marshall Mcluhan links French Revolution with the invention of print media:

"De Tocqueville, in earlier work on the French Revolution had explained how it was the printed word that, achieving cultural saturation in the eighteenth century, had homogenized the French nation. Frenchmen were the same kind of people from north to south. The typographic principles of uniformity, continuity and lineality had overlaid the complexities of ancient feudal and oral society. The Revolution was carried out by the new literate and lawyers."[1]

One more example quoted by Mcluhan in this book *Understanding Media*, which refers a minor social revolution in an Australian tribe. "When Australian natives were given steel axes by the missionaries, their culture based on the stone axe collapsed. The stone axe had not only been scarce bút had always been a basic status symbol of male importance. The missionaries provided quantities of sharp steel axes and gave them to women and children. The man had even to borrow these from the women, causing a collapse of male dignity. A tribal and feudal hierarchy of traditional kind collapses quickly when it meets any hot medium of the mechanical, uniform and repetitive kind."[2]

While Mcluhan believes that Media possess the powers to change the way mankind lives and thinks, Joseph Klapper and other believe that "media reinforce existing values and attitudes."[3] Ultimately, reinforcement is also a kind of change in the way of life.

Long long ago, before the spoken word was formed, human species must have communicated by roaring, crying or gesticulating. "And out of these sounds and, in very slow measure, must have emerged sounds which were identified with objects, animals and trees, and action of all kinds, then thoughts and deeds and feelings."[4] It is very difficult to say, when the spoken word was formed but the formation of word was definitely the beginning of the civilisation of the human race. Later speech and languages must have been developed depending on the needs and requirements of the races in different parts of the world. And "then, into this mode of composition came the new influence of writing. As to how it came in – that is all speculation. Early inventions often spread slowly and unevenly...We may guess perhaps that here was a final stimulative effect before the scribes and the editors took-over, and speech, the living voice, gave place to the text and the books came to the throne."[5] And then came the invention of printing, which was the major revolution of the time. The speed of these transformations was very slow and took long years of sustained development.

The speed of new inventions was geared up from the nineteenth century when number of new extensions were developed like steam engine, railways, road transport, telephone and wireless telegraphy. If the nineteenth century was the period of Industrial Revolution, the beginning of the twentieth century was the period of revolution in Mass Communication. The invention of Radio and Television brought major and speedy revolution in the world which made it possible to communicate the message in a broader way to the masses in no time. The rapid and faster growth of these electronic media made a different type of man on the earth. The effect of any media of communication on the society is definite whether slow or fast.

"The medium of money or wheel or writing, or any other form of specialist speedup of exchange and information, will serve to fragment a tribal structure. Similarly, a very such greater speedup, which occurs with electricity, may serve to restore a tribal pattern of intense involvement such as took place with the introduction of Radio in Europe, and is now tending to happen as a result of TV in America."[6] wrote Mcluhan, and this is what says Luthra, "The coming of radio has been described by the social scientists and thinkers as the dawn of a new age, much the same way as the invention of the wheel, the printing press and steam locomotion had been seen to mark important stages in the progress of mankind."[7]

The invention of radio in itself was a great event particularly when the process of nationalism was in its full swing. "The internationalism of the inventive process in wireless history was the necessary prelude to the nationalism which has expressed itself in the creation of broadcasting institutions. Few national traditions, national way of life, and national policies. The initial internationalism was expressed quite simply in the varied nationalities of the leading inventors."[8] The radio as broadcasting institution became a public service and its impact on the society was faster than any other means of mass communication. The impact has been well expressed by Asa Briggs, the writer of 'The Birth of Broadcasting' : " Broadcasting was of the greatest possible importance in relation to this changing social pattern. It arrived at a time when many different social forces were converging. Would it augment and accelerate the tendencies described above or would it seek to counteract and check them? ... Would it mould or could it merely distract? The questions were basic, although in 1918 there was no one to ask them."[9]

In the early days when broadcasting was in its experimental stage, speculations and doubts about the effects of this new invention on the society were quite natural. Speculations started emerging about its impact on other mode of communications like concert halls and readers. "What is less frequently remembered is the debate about the likely social effects of broadcasting, which has much in common with the recent debate about the likely social effects of television. Broadcasting, it was claimed, would not only keep people away from the concert halls, it would stop them from reading books. It would encourage contentment with superficiality. 'Instead of solitary thought' the headmaster of Rugby complained,'people would listen in to what was said to millions of people, which could not be the best thing, '(Quoted in the Daily Telegraph, 23rd October, 1926.)"[10]

Reactions and counter reactions were quick and instant. However, doubts were soon cleared when broadcasting was started on regular basis.

"Lord Ruddell, a voluble but on the whole reasonable friendly critic of broadcasting, conveniently catalogued many of the leading questions in Dec.1923. His article was significantly called 'Modern Witchcraft.' What effect is radio going to have on life? ...Are people going to read less? Are they going to talk less? Are they going to be better or worse informed? Are they going to the theatre and music less? Are those who reside in rural districts going to be more or less satisfied? Who can tell?..So far as the present generation is concerned, I believe that those accustomed to read and who like reading will continue to read whether they use the radio or not. But what about the next generation brought up on radio? Are they going to prefer information through the medium of the ear to that through the medium of the eye."[11]

Simultaneously, cinema was also emerging as a powerful medium in those days which was a big challenge to the theatre. It was also feared that theatre and press will be losing their hold due to broadcasting but these views proved to be speculations:

"Entertainment thrived, as did the entertainment industry. The main challenge to the theatre was coming from cinema, not from the BBC. The press was not losing its hold on the public.

It was a pressman, Sir Robert Gray, who wrote in the Radio Times in July, 1926 that 'Supposing that listeners receive a larger service of news it does not follow that the press will suffer to any appreciable extent.' The sale of books was increasing, and more than one local librarian in his annual report referred to wireless an a 'new ally ..... creating and deepening the interest of the public in the higher forms of literature.' The beginning of a popular revolution in musical appreciation was generally conceded. Conclusions about the effect of radio on children and the home were remarkeably similar to recent conclusions about the effects of television."[12]

The impact of the wireless media like radio is quite different from the other means of communications like telephone, cinema, press, etc., as B.N. Ahuja in his book, *Mass Communication* explains:

"Electronic media is of great value as it can reach millions at home, overcoming the barriers of illiteracy. Electronic media does not depend on the communication through roads or wires for reaching their target. The wireless media teaches each and every person without the need of urbanisation and overcrowding the cities. Among the various media, however the newspaper continue to be the most powerful, although it is less direct than the broadcast media and less intimate. Between Radio and television on the one hand, the film on the other, the difference is that radio and television are more capable of providing an immediate impact, whereas the reaction of a motion picture may be remote except in the spheres of social life."[13]

Radio has been classified as Hot medium by Marshall Mcluhan. "There is a basic principle that distinguishes a hot medium like radio from a cool one like the telephone, or a hot medium like movie from a cool one like Television. A hot medium is one that extends one single sense in 'high definition'. High definition is the state of being well filled with data."[14]

B.N.Ahuja has given six reasons, justifying the superiority of broadcasting over other medium of communications: (Three of them are given below):

"First, broadcasting is extremely popular with the public and attracts a larger audience than any other mass medium in history, both relatively and in absolute numbers. In some individual cases, both radio and television seem to be truely addictive.

Third-during a period of increasing population, prosperity and literacy, newspapers has not increased in number....

Sixth-broadcasting has become a part of ordinary living in contemporary society in a way that no other mass medium or art form has approached. Television or radio are in the home, in the car, in the office, on the beach, on the street and constantly in company with a majority of the population. Broadcasting is about as ubiquitous as printing and for some people is a far more intimate and constant companion. The theatre, pictorial art, and either contemporary of classical literature, none of them are a part of everyday living for most people:- they are not really an element of our communal experience. Not even the newspapers are a component of our common culture in the sense that broadcasting has become."[15]

Radio provides person to person communication – says Marshal Mcluhan:

"Radio affects most people intimately, person to person, offering a world of unspoken communication between writer, speaker and listener. That is the immediate aspect of radio. A private experience. The subliminal depths of radio are charged with the resonating echoes of tribal horns and antique drums. This is inherent in the very nature of this medium, with its power to turn the psyche and society into single echo chamber."[16]

In different field studies which were made to collect sociological dates, it has been confirmed that the radio is significant as altering device, and is effective for dissemination of information. In India where percentage of literacy is very small, the radio has played an important role in entertaining, educating and informing people at the lowest cost. Radio programmes have made direct impact on the society. Rural programmes were useful in getting farmers to adopt new methods of cultivation and increase their production. Similarly in other fields like entertainment and music programmes, role of radio is unique.

Similar impact has also been observed in the field of creative art. "Broadcasting shares the characteristics of creative art with other intellectual and aesthetic persuits..."[17] wrote Mehra

Masni in *Broadcasting and the People.* "If the invention of writing brought about a minor revolution in communication, the invention of printing brought about a major one."[18] said Narayan Menon in *The Communication Revolution*, but the intensity of revolution brought by the broadcasting was beyond expectation, "Of course every opinion expressed on these subjects generated counter opinions. There would be more reading of books and certainly more buying of music, 'In five years time', wrote one famous musical scholar in October, 1923, 'the general musical public of these islands will be treble or quadruple in its present size'. (*Ibid.*, 19 Oct. 1923)"[19]

Radio in the field of education and music played a marvellous role in the standardisation and unification of the norms. Asa Briggs expressed his views in his book *The Birth of Broadcasting* about the influence of BBC in Britain, "The influence of the BBC both on education and the pronunciation of 'Standard English' has been noted by almost all the people who have described its work. In music too there was a parallel influence, which illustrates in concrete terms Reith's view that the 'great audience' was not to be fed on the basis of today's statistics but created more seriously as large number of poeple, some of whom at least were capable of developing new tastes. 'Music for all was to be provided, for music was the common property and common enjoyment of mankind' (Broadcast over Britain-page 173). Getting everyone interested in music, however, was far more difficult than, providing music for all; 'for years the man in the street has been content to be pleased with music which is easily and quickly assimilated, and therefore not always of the best' Had the BBC allowed itself to be alarmed by complaints received against the playing of 'good music', had it been granted to the computations of a precocious 'Tam or Trendex' system, not only would broadcasting have failed to appeal to existing music lovers but 'disastrous havoc would easily have been wrought in the growing music taste.'(*Ibid.*, pp. 174-5). All this was obvious enough in 1925."[20]

In India, it was a matter of coincidence that the radio emerged as an effective medium, when the music system in North India was passing through a crucial stage. It was a period of codification and standardisation. The musicians and singers were not respected in the society and middle class families did not allow music to enter their homes. A period of great stress and strain. "The sociological factors had relegated the art, more or less completely to the dancing girls and their Ustads."[21] wrote Mr. Awasthy, in *Broadcasting in India*, the first published material on broadcasting in India.

Music in India is deeply rooted in the hearts of the millions of Indians. It is an integral part of daily life and there are songs and folklores which are associated from the birth to death of every Indian, whether it is a social function or religious practice. Inspite of the fact that India has number of diversities, languages and dialects, the traditions of Indian music kept the entire land united through its culture. The religious ceremonies are almost of the same type. Vedic hymns are sung in the same tune, all over India. Indian Music was progressing almost on the same patterns till 11th century in the north and south.

There was no real progress in the second half of the eighteenth century and development continued to be retarded in the nineteenth century. The musicians and scholars who were driven out from the court of Delhi took shelter in some of the States of Central India. Many died due to hardship and starvation, however, princes of Central India provided them encouragement upto a limited extent. There developed new diversities due to the isolation of musicians. During this period, different Gharanas/Schools of music were established by the musicians and Ustads of different states, while living in isolation.

British period is said to be the worst for the progress of Indian Music as stated by Pt.V.N. Bhatkhande:"In the early British period, music came to be more or less confined to courts of the leading native princes. The Europeans, as a general rule, looked upon it as semi-barbarous. I am aware, several Oriental Scholars like Sir William Jones, Dr. Griffiths and others made some attempts to study the subject, but their interest in it was not more than academic or antiquarian ... "[22] Further: "Under British rule, Indian Music did not get any special patronage from the Government, for obvious reasons, and the necessary consequences was that it commenced to deteriorate both, in quality and quantity".[23]

Before the invention of broadcasting, listening music, while relaxing at home was amazing. It was unbelievable to listen music without musicians and musical instruments:"I didn't believe" wrote Clayre & Alasdair, in Impact of Broadcasting, "then, you see; I said it was impossible for us to sit in a room and hear music, then the music wasn't there. And when they tried to say it would come through air, well I just thought he was pulling my leg."[24]

In India, where travelling and attending concerts is beyond the pocket of the common man, radio brought music in their huts, from the clutchs of Ustads.

Hence, development of broadcasting facilities in India played marvellous role by providing listening of music to the remote areas: "The services of All India Radio undoubtedly deserve credit for the culture of music."[25] Anna Sproule wrote: "Modern communication shrink the world. A radio can carry information where roads have never reached....[26] and Mcluhan also expressed similar views: "They danced entraced to the tribal drum of radio that extended their central nervous system to create depth involvement for everybody. 'I live right inside radio when I listen. I more easily lost myself in radio then in a book' said a voice from radio poll."[27]

In fact, Broadcasting in India inherited the traditions from BBC, at the time when broadcasting was invented and was at the experimental stage, India was under British rule. The earlier work in this regard was done by J.C.W. Reith, Asa Briggs, and Lionel Fielden, who are said to be the founder of the broadcasting institution. Their entire work gives history of broadcasting at the early stages. Data of sociological and cultural developments, history of broadcasting are the main features of these works. In later publications, the impact of programmes, has been discussed in detail.

Categorically, my work is related to study the impact of broadcasting on Hindustani Music, on its quality and quantity both. As evident from the figures, more than 40 per cent of the total programme composition is devoted to music items. Indian Music is also broadcast from the number of other countries of the world. Nowadays our traditional classical music is gaining popularity in several other countries and number of our great masters are regularly invited to perform abroad. Pt. Ravi Shankar, Ustad Ali Akbar Khan, Ustad Alla Rakha, Ustad Amir

Khan, etc. are few, who popularised our music in Western and American countries in early fifties. Ustad Amjad Ali Khan and others continued the chain and number of Europeans and Americans became disciples of our great masters, and came to India, leaving their countries to learn and understand Indian Music and its age old tradition.

Our National Programme of Music is not only popular in India, but also in several other countries, overcoming the barriers of political boundaries and language. Eminent artists from all parts of the country are participating in this programme, and programme have a nation-wide listening audience, "in other words, it is a countries cultural ambassador to different parts of the world."[28]

Radio provided a platform to our professional artists, musicians, musicologists and young talent. There were some problems in the beginning, few of them were solved later. Problems and drawbacks are always there, whenever a new institution is established. If some problems are solved, several other follow, but institutions continue to run. There were reactions and counter reactions, merits and demerits, but it is not the fault of the system or organisation.

Radio as an institution, has not only provided a platform to pioneers, professionals and young artists, but also played a significant role in the formation of certain norms, without interfering with the traditions laid down in our classic Shastras. It would have been impossible to evoke the interest of the people towards traditional art form in such a broader way, without radio. The efforts of our great scholars would have been reached only to a limited amount of population who were having the medium of books, concerts and classroom lectures.

It will be appropriate to mention here that radio, although, has not produced any performing artist as such, created deep interest among the listeners and audience with its power of effectiveness. The impact of sound is direct and quick on the listener. "The elemental force, the expression, which lies behind the sound of a word is lost when it is spelt out on a page. It is this elemental sound which is behind the power of oratory, of declamation, and which affects the listener more directly than the meaning". Hence, it is the power of the sound which is important for a music system and not a written word.

Sound mediums like Gramaphone and Cinema, which emerged almost at the same time could only reach to a limited amount of population due to various social and economic factors. These sound mediums are run on commercial lines, hence devoid of any social or cultural approach or commitment. This void could only be filled by social or cultural institutions like Radio effectively. In the developing country like India, broadcasting is most suited media to the persuits of Indian musical traditions and "a powerful means of artistic expression," i.e. performing art.

In this study, achievements of broadcasting in the field of Hindustani Music have been discussed and assessed in terms of quality and quantity. The facts and figures about the number of stations, population and area covered, time devoted to music programmes, artists and listener's opinions and their taste have been reviewed and analysed periodically. In this regard, the experience of our pioneers and great musicians have also been shared. Audience Survey reports conducted by various agencies have also been analysed and examined with regard to development and transformation of public taste.

References

1. Marshall Mcluhan, *Understanding Media,* p. 14.
2. *Ibid.*, p. 24.
3. Keval J. Kumar, *Mass Communication in India*, p. 200.
4. Narayan Menon, *The Communication Revolution,* p. 10.
5. *Ibid.*, p. 14.
6. Marshal Mcluhan, *Understanding Media*, p. 24.
7. H.R. Luthra, *Indian Broadcasting,* p. 1.
8. Asa Briggs, *The Birth of Broadcasting*, p. 26.
9. *Ibid.*, p. 43.
10. *Ibid.*, p. 14
11. *Ibid.*, p. 15.
12. *Ibid.*, p. 16.
13. B.N. Ahuja, *Mass Communications,* p. 4.
14. Marshall Mcluhan, *Understanding Media,* p. 22.
15. B.N. Ahuja, *Mass Communication,* pp. 42-43.
16. Marshall Mcluhan, *Understanding Media,* p. 299.
17. Mehra Masani, *Broadcasting and the People,* p. 4.
18. Narayan Menon, *The Communication Revolution,* p.-15.

19. Asa Briggs *The Birth of Broadcasting*, p. 14.
20. *Ibid.*, p. 243.
21. G.C. Awasthy, *Broadcasting in India*, p. 36.
22. Pt.V.N. Bhatkhande, *A Short Historical Survey of the Music of Upper India*, p.34
23. *Ibid.*
24. Lord Windle Sham, *Broadcasting in Free Society,* p. 11.
25. Swami Pragyananand, *Historical Development of Indian Music,* p. 18.
26. Anna Sproule in Article *Window on the World* from Role of the Media, p. 36.
27. Marshall Mcluhan, *Understanding Media,* p. 298.
28. G.C. Awasthy, *Broadcasting in India,* p. 44.

2

Historical Perspective

A SURVEY OF THE FEATURES IN MUSIC BEFORE THE ADVENT OF BROADCASTING

The Indian Music has its deep rooted origin and centuries old tradition. A number of opinions about its origin are put forth. According to one thought, the Originator of Music is Brahma who handedover this art to Lord Shiva and Devi Saraswati received it from Lord Shiva. Devi Saraswati, the goddess of art, knowledge and music is called 'Veena-Pustak Dharini' in Indian mythology, who is worshipped even today by all alike without any distinction of caste and creed.

Another school propounds the theory that Lord Shiva created Rudra Veena by observing expressions of Parvati while asleep and sung five Ragas from His five mouths. Sixth Raga was sung by Parvati herself. It is said that when Lord Shiva performed 'Tandav'—the eternal dance–he was sorrounded by the gods (Devatas) and goddesses. Gods (Devatas) sung devotional song, Saraswati played Veena, Indra played Venu, Bhagwan Vishnu played Mradangam and the same was witnessed by Gandharva, Yaksha, Patang, Diddha, Sandaya, Apsaras and gods.

The writer of *Sangeet Darpan* Damodar Pandit also wrote that the Music (Sangeet) was first started by Brahma:[1]

"द्रुहिणेत पदक्विष्टं प्रयुक्तं भरते न च ।
महादेवस्य पुरतस्मार्गाख्यं विमुक्तदम् ॥"

Whatever may be the origination, it is evident that the folk tradition existed even before the Stone Age, "where folk used the string and bamboo as bow as their instrument."[2] The oldest book available in India as record is *Rigveda* where the names of several instruments like Mradang, Veena, Vanshi, Damroo, etc., are mentioned, and *Samveda* is said to be the Veda of Music:

"सामस्या गायंति" ।

Vedic Hymns were recited in three notes, i.e., Uddat, Anudat and Swarit, which is said to be composed by Ravana. Later all the seven notes were invented.

History of Indian Music can be divided into four ages:

(i) Vedic period (2000-1000 BC)
(ii) Epic age (Ramayan-Mahabharata) (1000 BC-800 AD)
(iii) Middle age or Moghal period (800 AD-1800 AD)
(iv) Modern age (1800 AD onwards)

The developments of Indian Music were almost on the same traditions in the entire India, till 1100 AD. With the invasion of Iranian rulers, the differentiation started. In Iranian system, there was 'Muqam' system similar to that in our Ragas. The Indian musicians, in those days, did not like their systems and norms to be disclosed to the invaders, and court musicians of those time popularised 'Muqam' system, which later called Mela or *Thhat* system. According to Amir Khusrou, famous poet and court musician of Khilji Gayasuddin observed, "People from different parts of the world came here to learn music, but after several years of their attempts, they could not have the soul of Indian Music."[3]

During the period from 1200 AD to 1600 AD, number of Pandits wrote in support of Muqam system. Few of them are:

(i) *Ragatarangini* – Lochankrit (1206 AD)
(ii) *Sangeet Parijat* – Ahobal (1560-1566 AD)
(iii) *Swarmela Kalanidhi* – Ramamatya (1509-1530 AD)
(iv) *Ras Kaumudi* – Shrikanthkrit.
(v) *Ragamala* – Pundreek.
(vi) *Raga Vivodh* – Somnathkrit.
(vii) *Chaturdand Prakashika* – Venkatmukhi.[4]

Even in South India, Mela system was developed due to the influence of Sufis.[5] *Swarmela kalanidhi* was the first book written by a south Indian Brahmin in support of Muqam system. He created confusions and did number of mistakes in classification of new 'Mela' or 'Muqam'. Once he quoted Sarangdeo for 'Hijuj' Mela. There are number of references mis-quoted by Ramamatya. So was the problem with other writers of that time. Each one had given his own view about the new composition.[6]

There was no unique and standard classification. In many cases same composition was quoted in different names in different books. "Even though, few scholars and musicians continued to follow 'Gram-Murchhna' system, for example, the artists of Gwalior."[7]

Refering to the period of Akbar, Pt. Ravishanker described in his autobiography *My Music My Life*:

"The period of almost two hundred years following Amir Khusrou is considered as the 'Dark Period' in the Northern Indian History. Wars raged continuously, and cultural progress came to a stop. But then, parallel with the Renaissance in fifteenth and sixteenth century in Europe, there came a reawakening in India's culture. In our musical history, the first outstanding name of this period is Raja Man Singh Tomar of Gwalior, who is chiefly known for his organisation of Druvpada style of singing. With the help of some of the great versatile musicians known as Nayakas, Raja Man revised the Druvpada style of singing, a development of 'Prabandh' singing and gave it new direction and shape.

Swami Haridas of Vrandavan was known as a famous saint-musician, yogi and singer during the early days of Akbar's period in the sixteenth century. Tansen whose name is famous as a great musician and singer in the Akbar's court was the closest disciple of Swami Haridas. Akbar's period was the 'Golden Age' in the development of Indian music system."[8]

He further described about the descendants of Tansen: "From Tansen descended two famous lineages of musical traditions (Gharanas), one sprang from his son Bilaskhan and is known as the 'Rababiya Gharana', because its members play the kind of 'Rabab' invented by Tansen. The other lineage seems from the family of Tansen's daughter Saraswati, who was married to a noted Been player, Misri Singh (who was later renamed as Nabat Khan, upon his conversion to Islam). This branch called the Beenkar Gharana, was named after the principal instrument its member employed, the Been."[9]

"Traditions continued to flourish and Sadarang-Adarang added new dimensions by improving Khayal style which existed in a raw form in the thirteenth century at the time of Amir Khusrou."[10]

In the beginning of eighteenth century, i.e., after Aurangzeb (AD 1707), there were ten successors of Aurangzeb (till 1857). During this period Indian Music continue to develop but not with the vigour it had attained during the preceding regimes. The reason given by Awasthy: "The puritanical Mughal Emperor Aurangzeb did not like the musicians and painters. They were not only thrown out of the court, but also driven out of the Capital. Many died of hardship and privation, but quite a few managed to find shelter in some of the states of central India, where they found new patrons among the princes, who provided them with both, means and encouragement, for the cultivation of music. But there was however no real development of music in the eighteenth and the first half of the nineteenth century. The musicians living isolated in distant states, deprived of mutual contacts, developed local and stylistic differences coupled with a rigidity of outlook."[11]

This was the period when number of schools (Gharanas) of music emerged in the different parts of Central and North Western India, with their own styles and interpretation. New styles of singing were also developed with their own peculiarities which suited more to the progressive and light music lovers. Sultan Gulam Hussain Sharki evolved Tappa style of singing, Khayal style was popularised during the period of Mohammad Shah Rangila by Adarang and Sadarang. Banaras and Lucknow are popular for Thumri, Dadra and Kajri styles.

There are some thirteen Gharanas (Schools) listed below: (for details-consult M.R. Gautam's, *The Musical Heritage of India*)[12]

(1) Qawwal Bache Gharana.
(2) Atrauli Gharana.
(3) Gwalior Gharana.
(4) Agra Gharana.

(5) Saharanpur Gharana.
(6) Sahasvan Gharana.
(7) Delhi Gharana.
(8) Fatehpur Sikri Gharana.
(9) Khurja Gharana.
(10) Jaipur Gharana.
(11) Bhendi Bazar Gharana.
(12) Kirana Gharana.
(13) Rampur Gharana.

There are other small Gharanas emerged by the offshoot of different Gharanas, but it is not found essential to mention, taking in view the requirement of the study.

Classification of Ragas was another problem during those days. Number of great scholars of different schools tried to form a code for classification and nomenclature of Ragas, but they differed from each other. While Gwalior school established by Raja Man Singh Tomar continued to follow Gram-Murchhna style, different opinions (Matas) were followed by different scholars.

Pt. Bhatkhande, in his paper read at the first All India Music Conference held at Baroda in 1916 stated:

"I shall proceed to notice some of the leading authorities of the last century now. About the Fasli year 1224, corresponding with AD 1813, one Mohamed Rezza (a noble man of Patna according to Raja Sir S.M.Tagore) wrote his work called *Nagma-e-Asaphi.* Rezza seems to have been thoroughly dissatisfied with the absurd and meaningless Raga-Ragini-Putra classification of his time and took it into his head to introduce some sort of intelligent principle in them. He boldly criticised all the four Matas (Viz: Bharat Mata, Hanumana Mata, Kallinatha Mata and Someswara Mata) wrongly respected in his time, and pronounced them as entirely out of date and unsuited to the spirit and practice of the time, and then laid down his own Mata as shown on p. 28.[13]

The above norms are quiet different from the present Thata System. "During the same period number of other pioneers emerged to classify the norms of Hindustani Music. Maharaja Pratap Singh Deva of Jaipur (AD 1799 to 1800) called his own experts and Pandits and in consultation with them he made an

Raga	Ragini.
1. Bhairava	Bairvi, Ramkal, Gujri, Khat, Gandhari, Asavari
2. Malkaus	Bageshri, Todi, Desi, Suha, Sughari, Multani.
3. Hindsol	Puriya, Basant, Lalit, Pandham, Dhanashri, Marwa.
4. Ahei	Gauri, Purvi, Gaura, Trivan, Malshri, Jastshri.
5. Megha	Madhuagha, Gaud, Shudhasarang, Badhans, Samant, Sorath.
6. Nat.	Chhayanat, Hamir, Kalyan, Kedar, bihagda, Yeman.

attempt to get a standard work on Hindustani Music written. The work was named as *Sangeet Sara*. Another important book written in the nineteenth century was *Sangeet Raga-Kalpadrum* by Krishnand Vyas. The book was published at Calcutta in 1842."[14]

Thus from the fourteenth to nineteenth century, Indian music passed through the process of classification. However, the British period of nineteenth century did not provide any special patronage and musical atmosphere was limited to the courts of native princes and private concerts. Europeans did not give much importance nor provided any help to the musicians.

"Until about two or three decades ago the Hindustani music had fallen neglect. Even the native princes who in olden time showed a great deal of favour and sympathy towards it, under the new system of education they received, began to be entirely indifferent to it. The result was that the older race of musicians died away without leaving their best art to their descendants and representatives."[15]

Last two decades of the nineteenth century were the turning points in the history of Indian music. The birth of National Movement produced number of pioneers and scholars. Several musicians and scholars emerged to work together in order to unify and reclassify the old and unscientific codifications. The present 'Thata' system in place of old Raga Ragini system is the result of hard work and extensive survey done by Pt. Vishnu Narayan Bhatkhande. He travelled South and North Indian

States, consulted number of musicians and scholars, and evolved a new classification after studying the 72 Mela (Thata) of South Indian scholar Vyankat Mukhi. It is more scientific and unified system rather than the Raga Ragini System, popular in different parts of North India.[16] He also invented a notation system for Hindustani Music to enable the students and scholars to record the compositions of Ragas which is still popular. He also collected number of composition of 200 Ragas and recorded them. The work is available in the name of *Kramik Pustak Mala*.

He not only worked hard to bring a new unity in the theory but also arranged number of concerts and conferences in the different parts of the country in order to give extensive publicity all over India. The new system suited more to the musicians and scholars and accepted by most of the North Indian musicians.

Other pioneers of that time were Maharaja S.M.Tagore, Pt. Vishnu Digamber Palusker, Omkarnath Thakur, Shankar Rao Vyas, Atul Prased Sen and others who accelerated the process of social acceptance of music.

"In the field of music the tasks before the pioneers like Maharaja Surendra Mohan Tagore, Pt. Vishnu Digamber and Pt. V.N. Bhatkhande was primarily those of resuscitation of musical theory based on scientific research and examination of the standard works of the past. The pioneers also tried to discover and rediscover musical norms so as to bring new unity in the theory and above all to fight the stigma attached to the art and those who practiced it. Schools and colleges were established throughout India for teaching of music. This process of social acceptance of music was further accelerated by the opening of music department in the number of Indian Universities."[17]

In Bengal and Eastern India, Sir Ravindra Nath Tagore, Dilip Roy, Quazi Nuzrul Islam radiated the dynamic spiritual energy into the life of the nation. The popularity of Rabindra Sangeet which in the combination of traditional classical and folk music, had proved that the experiments can be made in the field of music to suit the taste of masses.

However, unaware of the movement and experiments made in the field of music the Ustads and dancers of North and Central India, particularly those of U.P., Bihar and Punjab, continued their teaching in their traditional manner.

"In other parts of the country, however, no such experiments were made and the teaching and propagation of music was in the hands of notable Ustads and regular institutions which specialised in the teaching of strictly traditional music. In U.P., Bihar and Punjab, the middle class did not allow music to enter their homes for long time."[18]

Broadly, this state of affairs in the field of music was due to the lack of communication between the scholars, masters and music lovers of the different parts of India. Although, there was lot of published material, concerts were also arranged all over India, but it could not serve the purpose due to the various sociological, and financial factors. And result was that middle and lower class families were kept completely away from our traditional art and its developments. This was the time when technique of broadcasting emerged in India in the first half of the twentieth century as an effective medium of communication.

HISTORY OF BROADCASTING (Pre-Independance)

> "Broadcasting — the transmitting of programmes to be heard simultaneously by an indefinitely large number of people — is a Social invention, not technical one".
>
> James Curran & Jean Seaton
> in Power without Responsibility.

A Social Invention

The technique of transmitting signals through 'Wireless Telegraphy' was invented long before it was recognised as broadcasting. 'Wireless Telegraphy' was used for transmitting the signals during the First World War (1914-18) in place of telephone for military purposes, and not to the general audience. It was only in 1920 when popular broadcasting was started in England and America followed by other European countries. Wireless in those days was regarded as little more than an experiment toy. Later it became a social institution for masses.

Jean Seaton in his book *Power without responsibility* — The Press and Broadcasting in Britain called it a Social Invention:

"Broadcasting—the transmitting of programmes to be heard simultaneously by an indefinitely large number of people—is a social invention, not technical one. The capacity to broadcast existed long before it was recognized. 'Wireless Telegraphy' was developed during the First World War for military purposes. It was used as a substitute for the telephone—but one with the disadvantage that it was impossible to specify the audience which hear the message." An American engineer, David Sarnoff, first saw the possibility of radio in 1916. "I have in mind a plan of development which would make radio a 'house hold utility like piano and electricity', he wrote- 'The idea is to bring music into the house by wireless."[19]

Even after the popular broadcasting had started, people did not pay much attention to his new invention. It was a historic occasion when "Northcliffe, a pioneer arranged a 'Daily Mail' concert as a promotion stunt. Dame Nellie Melba was broadcast singing from Chelmsford. A number of countries of Europe heard the broadcast and attracted much larger audience."[20]

A Social Revolution

"The emergence of broadcasting can be regarded as social revolution and was accidental. Nobody knew till the end of the First World War that a substitute of the telephone, one day, will become the household utility"[21] and will bring a great social change, in a shortest period of time. In fact there were number of social and political reasons which made this media a social event. World War First was the biggest. "It is a common place of twentieth century social history that World War has been the agent, or at least the catalyst of major change. What has been less noticed is the extent to which war time forms of organisation—born of the unusual conditions—needs of the moment—have created structural fossils in important areas of policy, surviving immutably in peacetime, but with no particular relevance to the post war period."[22]

Till the end of the Second World War, not much attention was paid to extend the broadcasting system. "Broadcasting and education provided interesting examples of this process. Both were drastically reorganised at the end of the Second World

War. In each case the most of a 'tripartite' division, based on a supposed hierarchy of talent. The changes represented a sharp move away from a view of society as an aggregate of individuals towards an official concept of particular groups with separate needs."[23]

Birth of Broadcasting

In England there were some problems in those days and regular broadcast of programmes started little late, although the inventor of the wireless arrived in London in 1896. "The Marconi Company was founded in 1897—The first 'broadcast' of music and speech was made by an American, R.Fessenden, in 1906. There were no 'triode' valves in use until about 1912. In December 1916 the American Radio and Research Corporation was broadcasting concerts two or three times a week. A ban imposed on 'amateur' radio in Britain on the outbreak of War in 1914 was not lifted until 1919. The first well-known American broadcasting station KDKA, Pittsburgh, went on the air with regular broadcasts in 1920. During the same year regular concerts began to be broadcast in Europe from The Hague. Also in 1920—in February—the Marconi Company began to broadcast from Chelmsford. Later in the year the Post Office withdrew permission for these broadcasts to be made."[24] This was the great obstacle in the way of regular broadcasts. "Difficulties were, of course, to be expected. What we did not expect, however, was that they would be deliberately created, and obstructions be put in our path from almost every conceivable quarter",[25] spoke Lord Gainford in his speech to the BBC shareholders on 21st Sept.1923.

However, in America, experiments on broadcasting human voice through wireless started much earlier. According to Asa Briggs, the first Radio programme in the history was broadcast on the Christmas Eve in 1906 by an American:"It was an American, however, R.A. Fessenden of the University of Pittsburgh, who in 1902 first used wireless waves to carry the human voice—over a distance of one mile. On Christmas Eve in 1906 he succeeded in transmitting both speech and music over a distance of several hundred miles. It was amazing to the wireless operators on the ships when they received music and speech in place of 'pips' signals on their sets ..... Many of them called to officers to come and listen, soon the wireless rooms were crowded. Next someone was heard reading a poem. Then there was a violen solo; then a man made speech, and they could catch most of the words. Finally, every one who had heard the programme was asked to write to R.A. Fessenden at Brant Rock, Massachusetts and many of the operators did. This was the first broadcast in history."[26]

There were other events followed in future. "One of the first successful attempt to transmit music and speech over a transmitter took place in 1915 when an American company sent out a programme from Arlington, a United States naval station, to the Eiffel Tower in Paris, nearly 4000 miles away. Europe and Britain lagged behind a little at this stage because of World War I. But a certain Captain H.De A.Donisthorpe assisted by his wife managed to provide a weekly programme of recorded music for troops in 1917."[27]

In Britain

Since India was under British rule, and broadcasting in India was started on British pattern, it will be appropriate to discuss the history of broadcasting in Britain in short.

"The first radio programme in England was broadcast successfully by the Marconi Company on 23rd February, 1920, from a transmitter at Chelmsford, and a regular service came into operation in November, 1922 as a commercial enterprise. J.C.W. Reith became its General Manager. The private company was transformed into a Public Corporation on January, 1,1927, with its first Director General, J.C.W. Reith, a man of commanding personality and tremendous efficiency," stated Awasthy "His contribution lies not only in building up an efficient, strong and independent public service in Great Britain, but also in doing his best to persuade the governments of various other countries to take broadcasting seriously."[28]

Story is little different as quoted by Asa Briggs: "On 14 February 1922 the first regular broadcast service in Britain was started from Writtle: it was organised by the Experimental section of the Designs Department of the Marconi Company. Their London station, 2LO, began its broadcast later in the same year on 11 May. In the meantime talks between the radio manufacturers and the Post Office had started .... The BBC was born during the course of these talks. Its first programmes were broadcast on 14 November, 1922, although the Company was not formally registered until 15 December 1922."[29]

Though, the radio broadcasts in America were started much early then in Britain, social revolution, in fact, started from Britain, where a company was formed as an institution. "A company was formed and grew, but with that information and growth something happened both to British Society and to British Government. Broadcasting, itself ceased to be a toy, an amusing novelty, an affair of 'stunts' (we would now call them 'gimmicks') and surprises: it became an institution. It affected people's way of thinking and feeling."[30]

With the introduction of regular broadcasts, its impact on the society was quick. People of Britain were thrilled with this new invention: "As The Radio Year Book for 1925 extravagantly put it 'when we first get the wireless set from the shop there comes the first thrilling moment when the set is to be operated and the family delighted with music. This, like the wedding day and the first ride on a bicycle, gives a thrill such as we seldom feel in this unromantic age."[31]

Reith's Approach

It was, in fact, the Reith's concept, his sheer intuition, who understood the significance of this social institution and converted the technical invention into an independent public service. He wrote in his diary, "....broadcasting was a potential influence, national and international, of the highest import. That it would have been a prostitution of its worth, had the service been used solely for entertainment in the narrow sense. That the informative, and educational possibilities must be recognised and developed; He hoped 'that sooner or later broadcasting would cross all paths and be recognised for what it was."[32]

According to James Curron and Jean Seaton; "Reith believed that the function of broadcasting was primarily educative: its purpose was to train 'character'. According to this view, your class of origin and what you learnt mattered less than how you lived and how you learnt. This principle was the basis for his programming policy. Men might be unequal but they could all try equally."[33]

Hence, most of the broadcasting organisations in the world adopted three objectives, Education, Information and Entertainment in their policy for broadcast.

Even the inventors of the radio did not expect the tremendous influence of the society: "Neither inventors nor businessmen, however, had any early idea of the social significance of what they were doing. Nor did the prophets," wrote Asa Briggs. Future studies have shown, the significance of this invention that it brought changes in so many ways: "The relationship between technical invention and economic and social change is a fascinating theme in itself, as far this study is concerned, it is the prelude to all that went afterwards."[34]

The progress in the development of broadcasting institution was delayed in Europe and England due to the First World War. While in America developments took a totally different course. The progress in the USA was faster than anything and "by 1924 there were about 500 stations in the country. Commercial broadcasting sets maximum audience as its main object." Wrote Narayan Menon... "The large number of stations which sprang up like mushrooms all over the country, the absence of any clearly laid down principles of sponsorship, the confusion of wave-lengths, all made it imperative that some kind of national control was necessary. So the Congress passed the Radio Act in 1927."[35]

As a General Manager of the British Broadcasting Company, Reith made pioneering efforts to establish close broadcasting links with India. "Reith was anxious even before Beadle went to Durban to establish close broadcasting links with India. He discussed this subject with Colonel Simpson of the Marconi Company as early as November, 1923; 'I should like,' he wrote, 'to organise Indian Broadcasting from here.' (From Reith's Dairy 27 Nov.1923). "In 1924 after consulting the Board, he approached the India office on this subject, and in 1925 the Viceroy." He worte in his dairy 'He failed. There is neither vision nor recognition of the immense potentialities of broadcasting, no ethical or moral appreciation; just commercialism.' It is an unparalleled opportunity for service in India, but they have let the change go."[36]

In India

The birth of broadcasting in India can be traced out to the year 1924, "when a private club, 'Madras Presidency Radio

Club, started a broadcasting service in 1924. Its range was only 8 kms. but it was surprising achievement in those days. This was only on experimental basis and could not continue beyond three years for want of funds. Another effort was made by the Young Men's Christian Association by opening a new station at Lahore. Simultaneously, the Corporation of Madras started a regular service from 1st April 1930, broadcasting music for daily two hours from 5-30 p.m. to 7-30 p.m.... The service continued till 16th June, 1938, when the Madras station of All India Radio came up with a 10 KW shortwave and .25 KW Medium wave transmitter."[37]

In fact, the regular broadcasting service was made possible much earlier in 1927 when private concern under the name of Indian Broadcasting Company Limited entered into contract with the Government of India and chose for its operation in two metropolitan cities, Bombay and Calcutta. "The Bombay station was inaugurated on 23rd July,1927 and Calcutta station on 26 August, 1927. Both stations used 1.5 KW transmitters which could be heard within a distance of 50 kms. However, broadcasting was a costly affair in those days. The total licences in force were 7775, and there was no means of collecting of licence fee. In January, 1930 the Company approached Govt. of India for monetary help and on 1st March, 1930 it went into liquidation."[38]

Government Control

In April, 1930, the Government of India took over broadcasting under its control and called it the Indian State Broadcasting Servive but closed it down on 9th October, 1931. It was only in May, 1932, after a period of trial and tribulations, the Government decided to bring broadcasting under state management.[39]

The period from 1932 to 1936 is said to be most important in the history of broadcasting in India when a planned approach was made to organise a regular broadcasting service. "The Government approved a special grant of Rs. 40 lakhs for development of broadcasting and a separate office of Controller of Broadcasting was set up. In addition to the Calcutta and Madras Stations, a third station was opened at Delhi and the number of radio receiver licences increased three-fold. The Indian State Broadcasting Service was given its present name

All India Radio (AIR) on 8th June, 1936. Since then, the broadcasting in India made rapid increase and number of licences increased from 10,872 in 1933 to 92,782 in 1939."[40]

Amateur Clubs

Simultaneously, number of amateur clubs and private institutions also continued their broadcasting service taking in view the public sentiments. "Amateurclubs continued their activities even after 'regular' broadcasting started. This was permitted presumably because, in the initial years, broadcasting was still in its experimental stage and the coverage of the few existing transmitters, left waste areas in the country unserved. In fact, authorities charged with the responsibility of developing regular broadcasting in the country was not hostile to the amateur clubs in area it was not in a position to serve with its own Stations."[41]

One such club set up by the 'Young Men's Christian Association' began broadcasting in 1928 in Lahore (now in Pakistan)... This amateur activity continued in Lahore till 1st September, 1937. All India Radio inaugurated its 5 KW medium wave transmitter in Lahore on December 16, 1937. In Peshawar (now in Pakistan) also broadcasting had started in 1935 with the help of Marconi Company who offered the Government of the North West Frontier Province the loan of a transmitter and few community sets on the condition that if the experiment proved successful, the Government would purchase the entire equipment. The Government of N.W.F.P handed over the station to the Government of India on 1st April, 1937 ....Allahabad obtained a licence in 1935 and the Institute put out programmes daily for one hour. These broadcasts continued till February 1949, when the Allahabad station of All India Radio was commissioned. An amateur station at Dehra Dun came into existence through the enterprising spirit of the Superintendant of the Doon and the public which raised money by voluntary subscriptions. The broadcast started on 6th April 1936, but had to be abandoned on 10 May 1938 due to paucity of funds.[42]

Princely States

The role of few broadcasting services commissioned by the states and princes was also of equal importance during this period. "The Mysore state setup a broadcasting station on September 10, 1935 which was styled as Akashvani. This name was subsequently taken over by the entire network of broadcasting in India and has replaced 'All India Radio' except in broadcasts in English and External Services. His Highness of Gaekwad of Baroda laid the foundation of the Baroda Broadcasting Station in 1939. At that time two stations were under construction at Hyderabad and Aurangabad under the control of the Government of His Exalted Highness the Nizam. Also, in the same year, the Government of His Highness of Maharaja of Travancore, decided to setup a 5 KW medium wave transmitter at Trivandrum. At the time of India's Independence in 1947, five radio stations located within the princely Indian states at Mysore, Baroda, Trivandrum, Hyderabad and Aurangabad were in operation. The Hyderabad and Aurangabad stations of Nizam became nuisance to the people and the Government of India when British Government relinquished power in August 1947 when and just before the final merger of the State of Hyderabad with the Union of India. After the Police Action, the two stations came under the administrative control of the Government of India."[43]

Let us review the history of broadcasting again since 1931, when the service was started on regular basis. It was second time in five years when the regular broadcasting started by the Indian State Broadcasting Service was closed down as it was passing through a great financial crisis. However, the decision of the Government to closedown the service caused widespread agitation. Taking in view the pressure of the public opinion, Government decided to continue the service for some more years. Government of India also took certain measures to increase the income. Import duty on wireless valves and radio sets were increased by 50 percent, with the result the income of the Government doubled, and developmental activities started in this field. G.C. Awasthy, quoted another reason." The reason was that in December 1932, the British Broadcasting Corporation started an Empire Service which gave a great fillip to the sale of radio sets among Europeans in India. The number of radio sets in operation went 16,000 at the end of 1934, an increase of 8,000 in two years. By 1934, the Government of India had come to the conclusion that it would undertake extension and development plans for broadcasting. P.C. Edmunds was appointed the first Controller of Broadcasting in 1934. It was decided to setup a station at Delhi."[44]

But the real extension work started with the arrival of Lionel Fielden of BBC who had taken over as Controller of Broadcasting in India. "His appointment marks the beginning of the co-ordinated development of broadcasting in India and several of the present day traditions can be traced to genius of Fielden. For drawing up a detailed development plan, Fielden felt the necessity of technical advice and in January, 1936, succeeded in procuring from the BBC, *ex-gratia* services of H.L. Kirke, toured various parts of the country and drew up plan in which emphasis was on the setting up of medium-wave transmitters. Kirke returned to England after five months, and was followed by G.W Goyder of BBC who came in August 1936, as Chief Engineer, Goyder did not fully agree with the scheme proposed by Kirke and was of the opinion that if medium-wave transmitters only were used, it would not be possible to cover more than a small percentage of the total area of India with the funds available. It was, therefore, thought essential first to provide a basic shortwave service in order to give at least a second grade service to the whole of the India and then to supplement this service with a first grade medium-wave service at important centres."[45]

The development that followed was on the lines of Goyder, and number of stations were commissioned during the course. "Delhi station went on the air on New Years Day, 1936. Peshawar station was taken over by AIR in April 1937 and Lahore station was inaugurated towards the end of the year. In 1938 two stations Lucknow and Madras were started followed two more in 1939, Tiruchirapalli and Dacca making a total of nine. The Service range of Delhi, Calcutta and Bombay stations was increased by installing Shortwave transmitters. This was the pace development till the dawn of Independence in 1947."[46]

Contribution of Fielden

To develop broadcasting as organised institution was not a joke in those days. There were problems at every step. Fielden wrote: "Painstakingly, I searched for a reference to broadcasting for surely, I thought, as problem after problem was unfolded, examined and placed on its appropriate shelf," 'but he was determined as he understood the potentialities in India,' he further wrote, "surely in this immense, sprawling illiterate, broadcasting could educate, unify and direct as no other medium could."[47]

All India Radio was Born

Indian State Broadcasting Service was redesignated 'All India Radio' on June, 8,1936, and credit for this goes to Lionel Fielden, he reffered to this 'apparently simple' change how the Secretariat opposed to any such proposal, and he decided to get the approval and blessing of the then Viceroy, Lord Linlithgow, without which he was shrewd enough to realise, he would not succeed.[48]

Some Important Events[49]

1. In 1937, AIR was transferred from Ministry of Labour to Department of Communication and in 1941 to a new Department of I&B which after Independence became a Ministry.
2. In 1937, the Central News Organisation came into existence, which is now News Services Division.
3. In 1939, AIR started broadcasting for foreign audiences, which is now External Services Division.
4. On 1-1-1936, the day on which Delhi station was commissioned, the English Journal 'The Indian Listener' was published which after Independence aquired new name 'Akashvani'.
5. The transmission in those days closed with 'God Save the King' and not by Jaihind.
6. Within the fortnight of its going on air Delhi station was able to bring well-known musicians like Fayyaz Hussain Khan, Vinayak Rao Patwardhan, Nasir Uddin Khan, Wazir Khan, Majid Bai, Hafiz Ali Khan, Abdul Aziz Khan, Bennkar Bandu Khan etc.

Indian Standard Time

Till 1936, Delhi station observed Delhi time which was half an hour ahead of the Indian Standard Time. The Calcutta station observed Calcutta time which was 24 mts. ahead of IST, only Bombay station observed IST. This was all difficult for the listeners in tuning different stations. Hence all stations maintained IST since February, 1936.[50]

Basic Plan

In 1944-45, after World War II was over, a plan called Basic Plan, was formulated in connection with the needs for expansion of broadcasting in India. "Besides Zonal programmes from Delhi, Bombay, Calcutta and Madras and extensive urban and rural services for whole of the country, the plan envisaged urban programmes in 19 major languages and rural programmes in 125 languages and dialects."[51] The number of radio sets also rose considerably. "During the year 1939 and 1947, the number of radio licences rose from 74,000 to 2,48,000. The total number of licences were 2,48,000 in 1947."[52]

Before Independence in 1947, there were in all 14 radio stations, out of which 9 controlled by AIR and 5 by Princely states.

Total station in India before partition

All India Radio	Bombay, Calcutta, Delhi, Madras, Lucknow, Lahore, Tiruchirapalli, Peshawar and Dacca.
Stations in Princely States	Mysore, Baroda, Hyderabad, Aurangabad and Trivandrum.

After partition in August, 1947, three stations Lahore, Peshawar and Dacca fell into the Pakistan territory and India was left with six stations controlled by AIR and five by princely states covering 11% population and 2.5% area of the country with its 6 MW and 12 SW transmitters.[53]

INTRODUCTION OF MUSIC PROGRAMMES, QUALITY AND IMPROVEMENTS

> "Broadcasting in most countries does not base its policy exclusively on pleasing majority. It is to the advantage of broadcasting to widen, if it can, the scope of listeners' taste....Thus we find in most broadcasting organisations that Classical Music gains a place which a majority vote would not

actually give it and it is undoubtedly true that the taste for classical music has in many countries, been considerably strengthened by this policy."

From the official report from the Controller of Broadcasting in 1940.

Music is the integral part of the daily life of any social system of the world. It is evident, that the programmes of every broadcasting organisation in the world included sufficient duration of music programmes. It is difficult to trace out record, however, the earliest programme composition of the BBC published in Asa Brigg's, *The Birth of Broadcasting*, shows that out of total programme composition, 73% time was devoted to music, out of which the classical music was 9.93%, in 1926. "Music and the drama are often linked together. Radio drama had made only limited progress by the end of 1926, although, there was talk even at this stage of the emergence of a new art form..."[54]

The first music concert in the history of BBC was broadcast on 30th March, 1926. "The last year's programmes of the 'old BBC' were more carefully polished than those of any previous year and a number of them stood out above the rest. What was generally described as the greatest musical achievement in the history of the Company was the broadcast from the Royal Opera House, Convent Garden, on 30th March,1926 of the first (concert) performance in Britain of Rimsky-korsakov's opera *kiesh*. On 20th September the first Gilbert and Sullivan opera was broadcast."[55]

Even in India, most of the broadcasting stations started their broadcasts with music programmes only, and 90% of the total broadcast hours was music.

But the quality of the music programmes at the listener's end was considerably poor and musicians and music lovers reacted voilently. "In the early days of wireless broadcasting musicians and music lovers reacted voilently to the broadcast of music programmes. They called it an 'abominable contrivance'. Their reaction is understandable. The technical equipment was still in its experimental stage and judged from the present standard microphones were primitive and acaustic treatment of studios poor.... The annoyance and anger of musicians is not surprising. What is surprising that in most countries this hos-

Programme Composition of BBC, for the month of October and November, 1926

Category	*Details*	*October*		*November*	
		Hrs.	%	Hrs.	%
Exotic Music	Ancient or Futurist	0.03	0.03	0.09	0.09
Classical Music	Opera	3.2		3.13	
	Orchestra	2.9		1.97	
	Chamber music	3.3	12.02	2.76	9.93
	Song Recital	2.0		0.89	
	Violin, cello Piano, recital	0.62		1.18	
Medium Music	Music which may please all tastes	7.42	7.42	11.86	11.36
Popular Music	Orchestra or Band with songs entertainers, instrument solo & c.	16.9		11.21	
	Musical Comedy	0.6		1.58	
	Revue	0.3		1.08	
	Star Entertainers Celebrity & c.	1.5	30.7	1.18	23.96
	Ballad Recitals	1.9		0.21	
	Restaurant-and Cinema Music, popular but unclassified.	9.5		8.7	
Dance Music		6.62	6.62	11.51	11.51
Drama	Plays etc.	1.7		1.69	
		0.8	2.5	1.67	3.36
	Other progs.	31.41	31.41	30.42	30.42
Gramophone records–unclassified		10.2	10.2	5.8	5.8
Theatre Ceremony	Outside Broadcast	Nil	Nil	2.07	2.07
Total Hours Broadcast		31 days, 248-75 hrs		30 days, 252.25 hrs.	
		Increase 4.5 hrs.			

Asa Briggs, *The Birth of Broadcasting*, p. 390.

tility persisted for long. Even after six years of broadcasting in Britain, for example, Sir Thomas Beecham, writing in November, 1928 in the Musical Times, was very vehement in his denunciation."[56] Quoted Mr.Awasthy, "Ever since the beginning of the present century there has been committed, against the unfortunate art of music, every imaginable sin. But all previous crimes and stupidities pale before this latest attack on its fair name, the broadcasting of it by means of wireless....The performance of music through this or any other kinderd contrivance cannot be other than a ludicrous caricature...If the wireless authorities were permitted to carry on their devilish work, in ten years time, the concert halls will be deserted.[57]

But successful efforts and improvements in the qualities of the equipments by the engineers made the broadcasting an ideal medium for music programmes. With the further advancements in the technique of acoustics, the performance behind the microphone in the studios, came out of the radio set with astonishing clarity and fidelity.

During the British time, the Europeans tried to infiltrate Western ideas of culture, education and customs into the Indian people and to depriciate Indian culture. The higher grade officers in AIR were either Europeans or were educated, and broughtup in the Western style. However, their success was limited to a small section of the urban society where they lived: wrote M.R. Gautam; "Gradually, chamber groups, trios, quarters, quintets- were formed in major cities like Bombay and Calcutta, Delhi, Madras and Bangalore followed suit. Some princely rulers of India like the Maharajas of Mysore and Porbandar were especially interested in Western music. The Maharaja of Mysore was a good pianoist and a reputed connoisseur. The Maharaja's sister was supposed to have specialised on the piano. This was indeed loudable trend. The presence of the British no doubt encouraged interest in Western music. Then the first radio station was founded in the late twenties while Indian music was the staple in the broadcast, a special section of Western music was also provided on a different channel in the peak listening period every day. Programmes were carefully and very well composed and presented.....Interest in the Western music, although it was restricted to the English knowing intelligentia—roughly 10 percent of the population—was not inconsiderable."[58]

Planning of Programmes

Let us also look to the other side of the coin, i.e. planning and timings of the programmes. "Broadcasting in those days (I am now talking of 1936-39) seems to me, was a service for the Sahebs" wrote Narayan Menon-"The service which was limited to eight or nine urban centres started late, 7 in the morning usually, in a country where people are earliest risers in the world, ... They close-down when the Sahebs and the officers set out for office and started again only when they returned home for their gin and lunch, after which the programmes close-down at 2-30 or so. The Memsahebs occasionally had a brief session round afternoon tea and the evening programme started about dusk. These patterns, with minor variations, continue to this day in some of the stations."[59]

In this connection Shri Girija Kumar Mathur, a well-known Hindi poet and former Dy. Director General of AIR, has expressed his memories in an article in Hindi Weekly-*Dinman*, which gives the real picture of indifferent attitude of broadcasters of those days; "The real leaders and patriots of the country were not allowed in the programmes. The great masters and musicians were paid a fee which was shamelessly low. The programme planners and policy makers were hardly acquainted with the traditions and culture of this land. They were brought-up in a purely European culture. They knew either English or Urdu."[60]

Music Programmes

However, few efforts were made to introduce Indian Classical Music in those days, while the Controller of Broadcasting Lionel Fielden submitted a report in this regard:

(a) A rigid interpretation of rule of classical music by schools which hold that Indian music has reached perfection and that no departure from tradition should be permitted.

(b) The combination of light and classical Indian music and the encouragement to amateur singers in order that Indian music may, on the hand, meet the changing tastes of the people without fundamentally altering its character, and, on the other, be redeemed from the distaste associated with its present exponents.

(c) A definite breaking away from present standards combined with the adoption of notation and harmony.[61]

With this report, thinking on introduction of Indian Classical music was started. However, in the absence of any norm and policy for planning, production of music programmes and screening of artists, the main objective in those days was to keep the programme going. Directors and even Programme Assistants were always in search of new artist who could be brought to the studios for broadcast. Though the listening was considerably increased, it was limited to the higher and privileged class who could afford radio set.

It is, however, important to discuss about the progress made in the field of music during pre-Independence period. In 1940 when Lionel Fielden could meet the Viceroy to present the view point of AIR directly to the Head of the State, A.S.Bokhar was appointed as Director General of AIR and the progress made in this field may be regarded as 'slow' due to the number of factors, and political unrest, absence of policy directives, and impact of Western Music are the main.

The first official report of the Controller of Broadcasting was published in 1940 in which much emphasis was given for music programmes:

"....The chapter on Music began with the statement that since music must necessarily fill about seven-eight of any broadcasting programme, it was naturally a factor of considerable importance."[62]

But the controversy was on the proportion of light and classical music. No doubt, light music is liked mostly by common listeners, it does not mean that the classical part of it should not be taken into consideration. It was stated in the report that : "Broadcasting in most countries does not base its policy exclusively on pleasing the majority. It is to the advantage of broadcasting to widen, if it can, the scope of listener's taste.... Thus we find in most broadcasting organisations, that classical music gains a place which a majority vote would not actually give it and it is undoubtly true, that the taste for classical music has in many countries, been considerably strengthened by this policy."[63]

Still, there were lot of problems over broadcasting Indian Classical Music over AIR, particularly Hindustani Music, due to various reasons and lack of standardisation in musical traditions. "The overall picture was that while musical traditions and taste for music were well established in South India, Bengal and Maharashtra, the same could not be said for North India where most of the musicians belonged to a professional class which was thought disreputable and female singers were identified in a popular mind with professionals and 'nautch girls'."[64]

The artists were not taking broadcasting seriously. "The professionals too were a little slow in taking to radio- especially those among the top musicians. For one the fee offered was not attractive enough."[65]

In those days, the 'mood' of the artist during the performance depended mostly on the appreciative response given by the audience. The artists were used to perform before the audience and the response was a deciding factor for the quality and duration of the performance... it was unusual for them not to sing or play to an audience whose appreciative response would sustain their interest or 'mood' and then the tyranny of specified duration for each sitting put them off."[66]

Both, the artists and AIR were facing the problems created by the new invention. The advance planning of the programme, where artist was suppose to declare the name of the raga to AIR authorities, never suited the artists, particularly to Ustads who were habitual to keep the secret till the commencement of the programme, "because the centuries old tradition with them had been to sing whatever they fancied at the moment,"[67] wrote Luthra, "However, the publicity which a performance over the radio brought them and the respect with which they were treated by AIR staff (who were continually enjoyed upon their seniors) to regard the artists as invited guests and not paid performers, gradually broke down their resistance and inhibitions about taking part in radio programmes."[68]

This was the time, when the initial efforts to organise classical music programmes were started; "In May, 1938, one Mr. Kristic, wrote to Fielden suggesting that a conference of competent musical critics be convened to advise on policy for music broadcast. Fielden discounted this idea and wrote back saying that such meeting was not likely to lead AIR anywhere in view of sharp divergences between the various schools of Indian music. He, however, wrote to Tagore, asking for his advice whether it would be advisable for AIR to have experts to direct music programmes and if so would such persons be available on a salary of say Rs. 500/- to 750/-. Tagore in reply expressed the view that it would be impossible for any one person to act as Director of Music for the entire service and suggested that AIR employ four Indian Music Directors— one each for North-South, Bengal and Bombay."[69]

In December, 1939, the Controller of AIR wrote to the Government suggesting that instead of creating four posts of Director of music as suggested by Tagore, the Programme Assistants in charge of Music at the stations should be given a grade of Rs.150-25-500 (instead of 150-10-250). Names of men like Rafique Gaznavi, Anil Biswas, Timir Baran, Keshav Rao Bhole and others were considered but it was seen that they were already earning higher wages in films.

This shows that efforts to organise the music department of AIR were made in an unorganised manner. "Audition, as a matter of course, were arranged by the Programme Assistants in charge of music and generally heard by at least one other senior officer, such as Assistant Station Director or Station Director. One doubts, if there is a notable artist today who had not been discovered by AIR before the much vaunted Audition system came into operations.[70] It will be appropriate to mention here that "at that time, Ali Akbar Khan was working as a Staff Artist (Sarod Player) at the Lucknow station on Rs.150/- per month."[71]

Further, in 1941, the Station Directors were asked to suggest the names of the musicians who could assist the Station Director in planning and production of music programmes, "Prof. S.N. Ratanjanker was also requested by the Directorate to give a list of music journals, Universities of important music schools and organisations and has degree course in music. The idea being to know about from where such people could be recruited. Among those appointed thus were Prof. B.R. Deodhar at Bomaby, Dr. Sachin Das Motilal and Smt. Bijon Ghose Dastidar (at Culcutta)."[72]

Light Music

Side by side, efforts were also made to improve the quality of light music programmes. "A suggestion about preparation of new type of light music as a measure to counterblast bad film music was discussed at the Station Director's conference in October 1943 and the matter was followedup later with heads of Bombay, Calcutta, Madras and Delhi stations. Victor Paranjoti then Station Director Calcutta suggested the creation of a Unit to prepare one light 'song of the week', as an entirely new composition, sung by a first class artist, and to go on plugging the sung once everyday for a whole week', this will give a repertoire of 52 songs every year'. The Madras and Tiruchy stations had earlier in 1942, reported on their efforts in creating new type of good light music 'genuine and true to our tradition in the place of cheap hybrid music which threatened to catch the masses and ultimately menaced out musical culture."[73]

With their limited resources, stations of South India reported first in creating new type of light music based on purely Indian traditions. "Under the title 'Na Chapi Kavyam Navamitya Vadyam', taken from Kalidasa, the Madras station started a weekly programme of new songs every Wednesday at 7:45 p.m. from January 1, 1943 with the well-known singer Vasundhara Devi providing the Vocal refrain. The Gramaphone Co. Ltd. Dum Dum who were asked for estimates for pressing commercial discs of these songs. Nothing came of this proposal in the end and the experiment could not be sustained beyond December 1943, because of the Stations' difficulty in rehearsing etc. by an overworked orchestra and lack of good voice for the vocal part."[74]

If this scheme could have been materialised, it was possible to keep the record of the good compositions of those days and repetition of such good music from various stations, would have been definitely a great achievement in diverting the taste of masses from cheap music to our traditional music.

Indo-Western Music

Experiments in the field of Indo-Western music were also carried out with a great success. A reference from the 'Indian Broadcasting' will give us an idea about progress. "....another experiment, that of Indo-European Music which was initiated by John Foulds, Director of Western music at Delhi, who alongwith Walter Kaufmann (who held a similar position at Bombay station, and who will be long remembered for composing AIR's signature tune), did a great deal to organise good quality of Western music broadcast from the stations on regular basis. In a letter of June 27, 1943, Kaufman wrote to Bokhari (Controller of Broadcasting) from Bombay that he had removed all the bad artists from the station's programmes and made Mehli Mehta (who was an income tax man) into a useful violinist."[75]

There was still a problem for the Indian artists in participation of Western music programmes and that was of Staff notation system. Most of the Indian artist could not follow the same as they were habitual to remember the tunes as done in the case of ragas and light music. "In October 1942, it was decided at the Station Director's conference that staff notation be taught to AIR's instrumentalists so that experiments in orchestra and harmony could be tried out. Classes for this purpose were held at some of the stations with varying degrees of success. Z.A. Bokhari, SD, Bombay wrote frankly to the headquarters in July 1946 that none of the artists employed at this station would benefit by such lessons."[76]

Fould's Approach

Foulds did a great deal in introducing harmonical compositions, based on purely Indian ragas and for that he also trained Indian artists to follow the Staff notations but with a less success, as the Indian artists are habitual to remember the tunes and compositions by heart. "Foulds was fascinated with the idea of introducing harmony into Indian music and the AIR Orchestra conducted by him gave a public concert in 1938 at Regal Theatre in Connaught Circus, New Delhi with the Viceroy and Lady Linlithgow as the Chief Guests. Indian instrumentalists had been trained to read staff notations for this purpose, although some of them confessed later that they knew the music by heart and only pretented to look at the printed score really."[77]

AIR can never forget Foulds for his outstanding work in bringing together the Indian and Western music. His idea was later experimented by other Indian musicians like Pt. Ravi Shanker, Yemini Shanker Shastry, Timir Baran in composing the Vadya Vrind. "He was well known in Europe, and his 'Essays in the Modes' published in 1928 has attracted a good deal of attention as an attempt to harmonise the pure modes of Indian music in a manner worthy for their beauty and importance."[78] The initiative taken by Foulds did a great favour in popularising Indian music not only among Indian listeners, but Europeans were also acquainted with the concept of ragas compositions. The light music listeners had also enjoyed the new compositions.

Banning of Harmonium

For banning the use of harmonium in AIR music programmes, in March 1940, credit goes to Foulds, ".....in an article entitled 'Harm-onium' carried in 'The Indian Listener' he described this instrument as 'Un-Indian' and 'Un-musical'."[79] The stations were directed to dispose off these instruments and not to use them in any of the music programme, even for rehearsals and providing 'effects' in plays or features. It is a fact that harmonium which is built on the basis of 'equally tempered scale' does not suit the Indian system of notation which is based on 'Shrutis'. It is really surprising that no Indian artist or musicologist had initiated the ban of harmonium. On the other hand, ban of harmonium was opposed by the number of artists, dealers and makers. Most of the artists opposed the ban due to the reason that this instrument covered the faults of their voices during the performance. "However, this move found support from many others, Tagore writing from Shantiniketan said that he had always been very much against the prevalent use of harmonium and that it was banished completed from ashram. Sir Raza Ali, a well-known connoisseur of music said he was not prepared to concede that harmonium was a musical instrument."[80] All top graded and established artist supported the ban. "Pandit Ratanjanker wrote from Lucknow expressing full support for AIR's move, and Dr. Zakir Hussain, then Head of the Jamia Milia Islamia, Delhi, said in his letter that he hoped AIR would succeed in persuading the public that it ought to be discarded. 'I cannot give any technical reason, but I have always felt that it jars on the senses because it is so out of tune with the spirit of our music'. Mr. T. Laxman Pillai of Trivandrum gave it as his conviction that 'harmonium' was incapable of producing what were universally known as the beauties of Karnataka music, such as 'Gamakas' and 'Shrutis'; 'The Indian Listener' in its issue of March, 22, 1940, carried a cartoon with the caption 'Herr Monium' and asked readers to tune in to the Delhi station on April-4 at 8-30 PM for a 'special programme' featuring the rise and fall of a dictator, thus giving a topical World War II touch to the publicity."[81]

Occasionally, pleas were made to lift the ban but "as far as AIR was concerned, the harmonium was given a fitting burial in March, 1940 and rested in peace for almost a quarter of a century"[82] Even after Independence, harmonium did not enter AIR studios till 1971.

This was 'all said and done' but so far the question of policy was concerned, there was no such concrete initiation. Decisions were taken by the individuals and not by the committees and penals. Sardar Patel as a Minister of I&B was too busy with the merger of Princely states. "Till 1947 the nature of programmes broadcast from different stations of AIR had a largely democratic basis. The likes and dislikes of the listeners in each area were taken into consideration in determining the final shape of programmes originating from each station. Such policy, while it produced programmes which were widely popular without being cheap, was also responsible for limiting the quantity of such programmes as were not acceptable to the tastes of the large majority in a particular area to reasonable proportions. For a broadcasting service which was still struggling to find its proper place in the hearts of people, such a programme policy proved sound and paid dividends in the form of increasing listeners."[83]

This state of affairs continued till the partition after which few well-known artists migrated to Pakistan, and dust of storm only settled in 1952, when Dr. Keskar resumed office as the Minister of Information and Broadcasting.

ARTISTS—AN ESTIMATE WITH HISTORICAL REFERENCES (Pre-Independence)

The continuous development of any art form, especially music, is always conditioned with the high sense of devotion and rigorous practice by its artists and scholars. The glorious traditions of ancient Indian music survived only because of the Royal Patronage by the Emperors, Kings and rulers of this land. It has, of course, altered and changed its phases over the years, but its basic thread appear to remain the same as it was thousands year ago. The tradition of patronage was continuously maintained from the earliest period of highly developed age of civilization. Gowri Kuppuswamy and M.Hariharan described in 'Royal Patronage of Indian Music':

"The continuous, full-blown development of any art, and especially the highly fluid art of music, is always conditioned by the strength of inducive principles of permanent and objective value. So far as Indian Music is concerned, it is our monarchs, who, enunciated, and stabilised by illustrative practice, the canons of this hoary musical system as well as the formative and directive principles determining its aesthetic and physical structure."[84] Further, "The Indian kings, the music stalwarts, have nurtured our music with tender care and have been its willing captives. In fact musical training formed an indispensable item of royal patronage. Many were the rulers of India who were profound scholars in the theory and practice of this art. Several of them perpetuated their names by bequeathing an imperishable legacy of scholarly musical treatise to posterity. Also, probably no where else in the world has royal patronage and encouragement to music been as continuous and rich as in India."[85]

The historical facts can be traced from Mauryan period (325-188 BC) where royal interest in the literature and fine art was visible. This sustained encouragement to music continued during Simga rezime (188-76 BC), Gupta period (320-413 AD) and later during the time of Vikramaditya when renowned poets like Kalidas and Aswagosha flourished. Pallava monarch was the great. Harshavardhana of Kanauj (606-647 AD) the patron of Bana, whose well-known work *Kadambari* is replete with reference to music. Chola kings (during 11th and 12th centuries) encouraged and nurtured musicians and other artists in many ways. Lochankavi, the author of *Ragatarangini* was the court poet of Rashtrakuta monarch Kirtiraja of Kashi (1160). Lakshmana Sena (1170-1205) was the patron of great poet Jayadeva, the author of *Gitagovinda*."[86]

"Sarangadeva, the distinguished scholar and musicologist was patronised by the ruler of Devagiri, Sarvajana Singhana when he wrote his well-known work *Sangitaratnakar* (1220 AD)."[87]

By the closing years of thirteenth century, Muslim influence on Indian music was visible. Amir Khusrow, the great poet, musician and musicologist was patronized by the Khilji Kings (1290-1320 AD), was also court musicians of Allaudin Khilji (1296-1316 AD)."[88]

"During the Mughal period, Indian music flourished and progressed in new dimensions. Babur (1520-30 AD) had a great love for music. Qule Mohammed Udi, Khwaja Abdulla Makhareed, Hussain Meer, Anju and Banai were the few of the prominent musicians in his court. Humayun (1530-56 AD) was also a great lover of music. He was a devotee of Sufees and patronized a number of musicians, few of them were Meer Qalander, Qasim, Kochak and Hafiz Sultan Rakhta."

"Indian music was fostered and nurtured by the Mughal Emperor, Akbar the Great. Tansen, Baiju Bawra were great court musicians of Akbar. He himself was a great devotee of music and not only enjoyed musical performances but also studied *Sangeetratnakar* of Sarangadeva, *Raga-sagar* was written in the court of Akbar, in which classification of ragas has been done."[89]

Similar traditions were maintained by Jahangir (1605-27 AD) after Akbar. He himself was a devotee of music and encouraged musicians and artists. He enjoyed Druvpad singing in addition to Gazals and Qawwalis. He studied the works of Bharat and Sarangdeva. Vilas Khan (son of Tansen), Chhater Khan, Khurramded Khan, Makkhu, Imraj Shauki were the prominent court musicians of Jahangir.[90]

Even Aurangzeb (1659-1707 AD) who is said to be the enemy of music by few scholars of history, was too a great lover of music. His decision to stop singing in the court was purely political. His personal residence (*Antahpur*) was always full of artists. On special occasions and festivals he used to distribute honours and awards. He himself was a musician. There were number of popular Druvpadas in the praise of Aurangzeb describing that 'Aurangzeb became Samrat (King) by the blessings of Brahma, Vishnu, Mahesh and Vyas'. During his regime, Faqeerullah, a Subedar of Kashmir, wrote *Raga Darpan* which was presented to Aurangzeb. A employee of Aurangzeb Mirza Roshan Zamir translated *Sangeet Parijat* in Persian. Both the books are preserved in the Raza Library of Rampur.[91]

This tradition of patronising continued till the fall of the Mughal Empire. The artists, musicians, musicologists and scholars, enjoyed the privilege and did a great service to nurture and flourish the Indian Music. Rigorous practice and continuous study, devoting whole life, leaving bread earning aside becomes the essential part of the daily routine, which is only possible when artists are patronised.

The invasion of Europeans was a crude shock to our art and tradition, in the eighteenth century. The structure of Indian society was totally destroyed by the British rulers. On the other hand, Europeans tried to spread their culture and in doing so brute force was also used, when the last Mughal Emperor Bahadur Shah Jafar, a great lover of music and art, was depressed and humiliated.

The socio-economic condition of the artists was falling rapidly. Most of the front rank artists did not allow their children to continue their involvement in the field of music due to obvious reasons. The artist who tried to continue suffered in many ways. Pt. Ravi Shanker in his autobiography *My Music My Life* described the hardship suffered by the great artist like Ustad Allaudin Khan Saheb:

"It was often frightening just to hear Baba talk about the hardship he suffered, as a young man in Calcutta. The little pay he received at the Star Theatre and occasional extra income he got by playing a recital here or there, all went to pay for gifts or offerings he brought to his teachers—fruits or sweets—in gratitude for their giving him lesson. Most of the time he had his one meal a day at some 'anna Chhatra', a food dispensary provided for the poor by some rich families ....The rest of the day Baba either went hungry or nibbled at a handful of chick peas and drank water of the river Ganges. He had no one particular place to stay. Sometimes he took a room in a cheap boarding house, and other times he stayed in a stable of a wealthy family."[92]

Pt. Ravishanker wrote his own sufferings in those days: "In the next few months I underwent the worst struggle of my life, both materially and spiritually. Many of the artists who had been performing in the India Renaissance Artists and who were now out of jobs were living in our house, and we brothers felt that we had a commitment to take care of these people and feed them for the time being, since they had originally givenup good jobs to join us IRA. Concert opportunities then were few...I was failing completely as an artist and as a person. Things had reached such a point that I had resolved to take my life."[93]

The condition of other artists was not different either. Laxmi Narayan Garg in his collection of biodatas of musicians and scholars *Hamare Sangeet Ratna* wrote: "Ali Akbar Khan was wandering here and there on the railway station without ticket and money, hungry and perturbed when a Bengali stranger met him. Khan Saheb told his story and first he was offered food then Bengali fellow managed few concerts at Khandwa. Whatever little money he got was enough to reach Bombay. In search of his bread, he went to All India Radio, Bombay."[94]

The history of our great musicians is full of adventures particularly during the British period. Bread earning was a great problem for them. They still continued their efforts devotedly at the risk of economic hardships to keep the art alive.

There is no such evidence in the history, that such efforts were in any way encouraged by the British Government. Scholars were doing on their own. Most of the institutions were financed by the native princes, who were the only source of encouragement. Pt. Bhatkhande in his concluding speech before the first All India Music Conference held at Baroda in 1916, requested native princes to help and patronize such events:

"Before concluding this address, I shall take this opportunity to express my immense gratitude to our noble and enlightened Prince and Ruler, His Highness Maharaja Saheb Gaekwar, who takes such keen interest in the matter and placed the whole of India under his obligation by his enabling us representatives to assemble here for this glorious work.....It is my earnest hope that the fact of this value will also be acknowledge by the other Native Rulers in this country by their making common cause with this movement and by their inviting the conference to assemble in regions under their rule in future years and that by this co-ordination of efforts, the last goal of general mass education in Music will be attained."[95]

The Ruler of Maiher state was a great patron of music who was influenced by Ustad Alla Uddin Khan Sahab. He invited Khan Saheb at Maiher and started learning music from Baba. A Music College was also established by the Maharaja at Maiher which was headed by Baba and so many great artists like Pt. Ravishanker, Ali Akbar Khan, Nikhil Banerjee, Timir Baran, Saran Rani, Pannalal Ghose etc. were trained at Maiher.[96]

"There are some more stories of sufferings of our great masters in those days: "Nissar Hussain Khan, a well known vocalist of Gwalior school was not having money even to go to Bombay. When he was thrown-out from the train by the TC, he started singing on the plateform and the crowd gathered around him.

During the period of Maharaja Jayajirao Scindhia, Khan Saheb was availing all the facilities in his court. After the death of the Maharaja, the management of the state came under a committee and Khan Saheb was then paid a sum of Rs. 50 in place of the facilities which he was availing during the regime of Maharaja. It was an insult to him and he left the court and joined the school of Vishnu Pandit (Father of Shanker Pandit)".[97]

"After passing fourth class, Pt. Omkar Nath Thakur, a pioneer of our music world, was forced to join a mill as a labourer for the sake of maintenance of his parents and brothers, still he continued his practice during these hard and difficult days. But obstacle could not alter his aim of the life and he was awarded. 'Padma Shree' on 15th August, 1955, i.e. after Independence."[98]

More or less, similar conditions were prevailing with the other outstanding musicians. (for detailed study, read biodatas in Laxmi Narayan Garg's *Hamare Sangeet Ratna*).

Though, few artists who were well off due to patronage of the rulers, most of the great masters were leading a life not worthy of their achievements. Socio-economic factors had taken the art to the dancing and singing girls, Baijis and their Ustads, with the result, in North India, musicians were not respected in the society.

Efforts were made to establish the social status by several pioneers, societies and institutions, but the approach of such institutions was limited and confined to a particular class of society. Most of the institutions were suffering from financial hardship and so was the condition of the artists in those days. The fruits of their efforts were visible only after 1952, when various awards and honours were introduced to honour musicians and pioneers. In this process, Radio has also played its role effectively, by introducing artists to millions of music lovers all over the country, thus providing recognition and improved their social status, which lead to economic respectability at a later stage.

References

1. Vasant Sangeet Visharad, page 15 (Damodar Pandit–*Sangeet Darpan*)
2. B.C. Deva, *Musical Instruments of India*, p. 2.
3. *खिलजी कालीन भारत,* पृ. १७९ "संसार के भिन्न-भिन्न भागों से आकर लोगों ने यहाँ संगीत की शिक्षा ग्रहण करने का प्रयत्न किया, परन्तु वर्षों के प्रयास के बाद भी उन्हें यहाँ का ज्ञान न हो सका ।"
4. संकलित-*मुसलमान और भारतीय संगीत,* आचार्य वृहस्पति, पृष्ठ ३९-४०
5. *मुसलमान और भारतीय संगीत,* आचार्य वृहस्पति, पृष्ठ ३५ "दिल्ली साम्राज्य के प्रतिनिधि मुस्लिम सूबेदारों की छत्रछाया में सूफियों और कव्वालों को दक्षिण में दूर-दूर तक फैलने का अवसर मिल चुका था । फलत: इन्द्रप्रस्थ मत अथवा मुकाम पद्धति का प्रचार-प्रसार सुदूर दक्षिण तक हो चुका था । विद्यारण्यजी ने इसी विवशता के परिणामस्वरूप मेल पद्धति या मुकाम-पद्धति का आश्रय लेकर उपलब्ध पचास रागों का वर्गीकरण किया था" ।
6. *मुसलमान और भारतीय संगीत,* आचार्य वृहस्पति, पृष्ठ ४५
   बड़ी मनोरंजक बात यह है कि इतना उत्पात करने पर भी रामामत्य कहते हैं कि समस्त देशी रागों में श्रुति, स्वर, ग्राम, जाति इत्यादि का नियम नहीं होता, परन्तु षडजग्राम का लक्षण तक न पाने वाले रामामत्य ने सभी देशी रागों को षडजग्राम से उत्पन्न कह डाला । पश्चाद्वती आचार्यों को इस दिशा में भ्रांत करने का उत्तरदायित्व रामामत्य पर है .... शारंगदेव पर अत्याचार की पराकाष्ठा तो तब हुई जब रामामत्य ने "हिजूजी" को ग्रामराग कहकर उसे शारंगदेव समस्त बता दिया । ब्रह्मा को भी संगीत रत्नाकर में हिजूजी न मिलेगा" ।
7. *खुसरो, तानसेन तथा अन्य कलाकार*–सुलोचना वृहस्पति, पृष्ठ ७५
   अकबरी दरबार के ग्वालियरी कलावंतों पर दक्षिण का कोई प्रभाव न पड़ा अपितु ये कलावंत अकबरी दरबार के विदेशी मुसलमान कलाकारों पर छाये रहे । अकबरी दरबार के प्रसिद्ध ३६ कलाकारों की सूची में तानसेन का नाम सर्वप्रथम होना और ग्वालियरी कलाकारों को विदेशी कलाकारों के पहले गिनाया जाना इस तथ्य का परिचायक है ।

   यह सत्य है कि पुंडरीक ने अपने ग्रंथों में उत्तर भारतीय रागों का वर्गीकरण मेल पद्धति से किया और यह भी सत्य है कि इस युग में अभारती पद्धति से प्रचलित रागों का संकर भी

हुआ । तथापि ग्वालियरी कलावंत मूर्छना पद्धति के मर्मज्ञ और संगीत रत्नाकर के परम भक्त रहे । मुगल बादशाहों ने इसी परंपरा के गुणियों को दरबार में प्रमुख स्थान दिया ।

अस्तु अकबर का दरबार संगीत रत्नाकर के रागों और तालों को भले ही पुनरूज्जीवित न कर सका हो तथापि बृजभाषा-ध्रुव पदों के शिल्प विधान पर संगीत रत्नाकर के प्रबन्धाध्याय में वर्णित 'धुर्वे' नामक प्रबंध के भेदों का प्रभाव भलीभांति था इस प्रबंध में प्रायोज्य पद ही आज ध्रुवपद कहलाते हैं ।

8. Pt. Ravishanker, *My Music My Life*, p. 49.
9. *Ibid.*, 50.
10. *Ibid.*
11. G.C.Awasthy, *Broadcasting in India*, p. 34.
12. Edited from M.R. Gautam's *Musical Heritage of India*.
13. Pt. V.N. Bhatkhande *A Short Historical Survey of the Music of Upper India*, p. 35.
14. *Ibid.*, p. 37
15. *Ibid.*, p. 34.
16. *हमारे संगीत रत्न*, लक्ष्मीनारायण गर्ग, पृष्ठ ९१-९२

"उन दिनों उत्तर भारत में प्राचीन राग-रागिनी पद्धति प्रचलित थी, और वहीं के संगीतज्ञ उनके नियमों पर ध्यान न देते हुये उन्हें गाते थे। बहुत बड़े-बड़े संगीतज्ञ जो कि गाना बहुत सुन्दर गाते थे। लेकिन स्वयं उन्हें इस बात का पता नहीं था कि यह गाना कौन से राग का है और इसमें कौन से स्वर लगाये जा रहे हैं । यह देखकर पंडितजी ने विचार किया कि दक्षिण पद्धति के जन्यजनक अर्थात् राग-ठाठ प्रणाली का प्रचार इधर किया जाये तो इधर का संगीत क्रमबद्ध होकर ठीक हो जायेगा अतः आपने ठाठ पद्धति प्रारंभ करने के लिये प्रयास शुरू कर दिये । फलस्वरूप उत्तर भारत के संगीतज्ञ राग-रागिनी प्रणाली को छोड़कर ठाठ प्रणाली को ठीक समझकर उसकी ओर आकर्षित हुये और कुछ समय बाद उत्तर भारत में ठाठ पद्धति चालू हो गई ।

संगीत कला का विशेष ज्ञान प्राप्त करने एवं उसके प्रचार का एक उपाय पंडितजी ने यह सोचा कि विभिन्न स्थानों में संगीत सम्मेलन कराये जायें । इस कार्य में आपको बड़ा परिश्रम करना पड़ा और सफलता भी मिली" ।

17. G.C. Awasthy, *Broadcasting in India*, p. 35.
18. *Ibid.*
19. James Curran and Jean Seaton, *Power Without Responsibility*—The Press and Broadcasting in Britain, Published at Methuen, London and New York in 1985.
20. *Ibid.*, p. 126.
21. Narayan Menon, *The Communication Revolution*, p. 27.
22. James Curran and Jean Seation, *Power without Responsibility*, The Press and Broadcasting in Britain, In the chapter Broadcasting- Social Revolution.
23. *Ibid.*

24. Asa Briggs, *The Birth of Broadcasting*, p. 20.
25. *Ibid.*, p. 143.
26. *Ibid.*, p. 27
27. Narayan Menon, *The Communication Revolution*, p. 27.
28. G.C. Awasthy, *Broadcasting in India*, p. 1.
29. Asa Briggs, *The Birth of Broadcasting*, p. 20.
30. *Ibid.*, p. 4.
31. *Ibid.*, p. 14.
32. J.C.W. Reith, *In To The Wind*, p. 99.
33. James Curron and Jean Seaton, *Power without Responsibility*, p.180.
34. Asa Briggs, *The Birth of Broadcasting*, p. 5.
35. Narayan Menon, *The Communication Revolution*, p. 29.
36. J.C.W. Reith, *In To The Wind*, p. 113.
37. G.C. Awasthy, *Broadcasting in India*, p. 3.
38. Publication Division Ministry of I & B (Edited version), *Mass media in India*, 1978.
39. *Ibid.*
40. *Ibid.*
41. G.C. Awasthy, *Edited versions from Broadcasting in India*, pp. 3-4.
42. *Ibid.*
43. G.C. Awasthy, *Broadcasting in India*, pp. 4-5
44. *Ibid.*, pp. 6-7.
45. G.C. Awasthy, *Edited from Broadcasting in India*, pp. 8-9.
46. *Ibid.*
47. H.R. Luthra's, *Indian Broadcasting*.
48. *Ibid.*, p. 192.
49. Facts edited from H.R. Luthra's *Indian Broadcasting*, pp. 92-96 and P.C. Chatterjee's *Broadcasting in India*, pp. 43-45.
50. Edited from H.R. Luthra's *Indian Broadcasting*, pp. 97-98.
51. G.C. Awasthi, *Broadcasting in India*, p. 11.
52. P.C. Chatterjee, *Broadcasting in India*, p. 45.
53. G.C. Awasthi, *Broadcasting in India*, p. 11.
54. Asa Briggs, *The Birth of Broadcasting*, p. 280.
55. *Ibid.*, pp. 389-390.
56. G.C. Awasthy, *Broadcasting in India*, p. 32.
57. *Ibid.*
58. M.R. Gautham, *The Musical Heritage of India*, p. 88.
59. Narayan Menon, *The Communication Revolution*, p. 31.
60. *दिनमान*, पृष्ठ ३३,-"उन्होंने एक नई शुरूआत की" विख्यात हिन्दी कवि और आकाशवाणी के भूतपूर्व उप महानिदेशक श्री गिरजा कुमार माथुर का एक लेख ।

"आजादी के पहले तकरेडियो एक अजीब किस्म के अधकचरे, १९ वीं शदी के पतनशील (डेकेडेन्ट) अभारतीय, घटिया सामंती सरपरस्ती के दौर से गुजरा था । यह अंग्रेजो हुकूमत की दासता के कारण ही नहीं था, बल्कि उसमें एक नई गुजरी अतीत जीवी, मध्ययुगीन मनोवृति थी, जो एकदम अरूचिकर थी । जो लोग ऊँचे और निर्णायक पदों पर थे वे पूरी तरह विदेशी जहनियत में पले थे और हर भारतीय चीज को न सिर्फ नीची, ह्किारत की नजर से देखते थे बल्कि उससे नितांत अपरिचित भी थे । वे सिर्फ अंग्रेजी और उर्दू जानते थे । अन्य किसी भाषा के साहित्य, साहित्यिक गतिविधि, सांस्कृतिक विरासत, जन-परंपराओं, आदर्शों से बिल्कुल ही कटे हुये थे । वे रेडियो के महत्व और "माध्यम" की गुणात्मक जरूरतों से परिचित तो थे, लेकिन उस वक्त तक पारसी थियेटर से मिलते जुलते जमाने में, या पुराने मध्ययुगीन यूरोपीय और फारसी कथानवग-अफसानों में ही सांस लेते थे । जाम और प्याला, साकी और मयखाना सिर्फ संगीत की सामंती महफिलों और मुजरों की अदायगी जैसे प्रोग्रामों में ही नहीं थे, वे असलियत में भी रोडियो की फिजां में फैले बसे हुये थे । सामाजिक समस्यायें, मियां बीबी के झगड़े, नौकर या मकान की तलाश तक सीमित थी । रेडियो के लोग लगातार अस्थाई रूपसे रखे जाते थे, ताकि कभी भी निकाले जा सकें ।"

61. G.C. Awasthy, *Broadcasting in India*, pp. 37-38.
62. H.R. Luthra, *Indian Broadcasting*, p. 298.
63. *Ibid.*
64. *Ibid.*, pp. 299-300.
65. *Ibid.*
66. *Ibid.*
67. *Ibid.*
68. *Ibid.*
69. *Ibid.*, p. 301.
70. G.C. Awasthy, *Broadcasting in India*, p. 38.
71. H.R. Luthra, *Indian Broadcasting*, p. 301.
72. *Ibid.*
73. *Ibid.*, p. 302.
74. *Ibid.*
75. *Ibid.*, p. 303.
76. *Ibid.*
77. *Ibid.*
78. *Ibid.*
79. *Ibid.*
80. *Ibid.*, p. 304.
81. *Ibid.*
82. *Ibid.*
83. G.C. Awasthy, *Broadcasting in India*, p. 30.
84. Gowri Kuppuswamy and M. Hariharan, *Royal Patronage to Indian Music*, pp. 1 & 3.
85. *Ibid.*

86. Edited from Gowri Kuppuswami and M.Hariharan, *Royal Patronage to Indian Music*, pp. 3-4-5 and 6.
87. Edited from the above pp. 4, 5, and 6.
88. *Ibid.*
89. *खुसरो, तानसेन तथा अन्य कलाकार*, सुलोचना वृहस्पति, पृष्ठ ७३-७४. बाबर का संपर्क ग्वालियर के कलाकारों से था, ग्वालियर के तानसेन ने *संगीत रत्नाकर* जैसे प्रौढ़ ग्रंथ को अकबर के विचार का विषय बना दिया था ।

    अकबरी दरबार में "राग दरबार" नामक ग्रंथ की रचना हुई उसमें तीन अध्याय हैं । इसमें "सारंगदेव" व रामाभात्य दोनों की चर्चा है । पुस्तक का संबंध अकबरी दरबार से हो चुका था । "राग सागर" में छियानबे रागों के ध्यान है, जिनके "उषावो" (हुसैनी) राग का ध्यान भी है ।
90. सुलोचना वृहस्पति, *खुसरो, तानसेन तथा अन्य कलाकार*, पृष्ठ ७४-८०

    "जहाँगीर संगीत रसिक था । एक ध्रुवपद के अनुसार जहाँगीर भरत के मत पर विचार करने वाला, सप्ताध्यायी (संगीत-रत्नाकर) से सुपरिचित संगीत के अंग-अंग में समाया और गुण ग्राहक था । जहाँगीर को ध्रुवपद-गायक भी प्रिय थे, वह गजल और कव्वाली भी सुनता था। तानसेन के पुत्र विलास खाँ, छत्तर खाँ, खुर्रमदार मक्खु, इमजान शौकी, उस्तान मुहम्मद इत्यादि कलाकार इसके दरबार की शोभा थे ।"
91. सुलोचना वृहस्पति, *खुसरो, तानसेन तथा अन्य कलाकार*, पृष्ठ ८०-८१.

    "उस युग में प्रत्येक मुगल शहजादे के लिये संगीत का ज्ञान अनिवार्य समझा जाता था अतः औरंगजेब भी संगीत-मर्मज्ञ था । औरंगजेब के अठारह जन्मोत्सव अंतःपुर में हुये थे । जिनके निवासी राग रंग में सवगिमग्न थे ... राज्याभिषेक के उत्सवों में औरंगजेब शायरों, मौलवियों और गायकों को पारितोषिक देता था । . . . फकीरूल्ला ने १६६५ ई. में राग दर्पण की रचना की । औरंगजेब के एक कर्मचारी मिर्जा रौशन जमीर ने "संगीत पारिजात" का फारसी अनुवाद किया । ये दोनों ग्रंथ रामपुर की रजा-लाइब्रेरी में सुरक्षित हैं ।
92. Pt. Ravishanker, *My Music My Life*, p. 52.
93. *Ibid.*, p. 77.
94. Laxminarayan Garg, *Hamare Sangeet Ratna*, p. 474.

    "भूखे-प्यासे आप स्टेशन पर घूम रहे थे कि अचानक एक बंगाली सज्जन आते दिखाई दिये । उनसे इन्होंने अपनी सारी राम कहानी कह दी । उन महोदय ने पहले तो इन्हें भर पेट खाना खिलाया और फिर शहर में सरोद के दो प्राईवेट प्रोग्राम भी करा दिये, जिनसे इन्हें बम्बई का सफर खर्च प्राप्त हो गया और ये बंबई पहुंच गये । रोजी रोटी की तलाश में अली अकबर आकाशवाणी बम्बई पहुँचे ।"
95. Pt. V.N.Bhatkhande, A *Short Historical Survey of the Music of Upper India*, pp. 50-51.
96. Laxinarayan Garg, *Hamare Sangeet Ratna*, pp. 471 & 245.

    "एक दिन आपके मन में आया कि चलो बंबई । दूसरे दिन बिना टिकिट के ही रेल में सवार हो गये । रास्ते में आपको टिकिट चेकर ने गाड़ी से उतार दिया । खाँ साहब उतर पड़े और प्लेटफार्म पर तानपुरा निकाल कर जम गये । वहीं पर आपने गाना शुरू कर दिया तो शीघ्र ही यात्रियों की भीड़ इकट्ठी हो गई ।

जब महाराजा जयाजी राव की मृत्यु हो गई तो उस समय राज-काज पंचों के सुपुर्द हो गया और पंच कमेटी ने व्यय घटाने की योजना बनाई, जिसकी चपेट में खाँ साहब भी आ गये । उनका और खर्च तो बंद कर दिया गया केवल 50/- मासिक ही दिये जाने स्वीकृत हुये । अतः निसार हुसैन खाँ साहब ने इस कमी को अपनी शान में कमी समझकर वह नौकरी छोड़ दी और विष्णु पंडित के स्कूल में आ गये ।''

97. लक्ष्मीनारायण गर्ग, *हमारे संगीत रत्न,* पृष्ठ 132.

''चौथे दर्जे की पढ़ाई समाप्त होने पर पंडित जी के हृदय में माता-पिता और भाईयों के निर्वाह का प्रश्न उठा, अतः कुटुम्ब की सहायता के लिये रसोई का और मिल में मजदूरी का कार्य करने लगे ।

3

Methodology

> "Research on relative effectiveness of different media of communication include (i) What role the media play (ii) How they motivate the people to bring about change in their value orientation and perception (iii) Which media are relatively more effective."
>
> S.C. Sharma in Media Communication and Development. (Quoting Wilbur Schramm).

Radio, as a broadcasting institution, is a medium of Mass Communication and the study of its impact on the society is a matter of research in Mass Communication. Hence it is important to understand, what is mass media and communication research, before the work is carried-out in detail.

"Communication Research, in the words of Wilbur Schramm (1957), is concerned with, how to be effective in communication, how to be clear, how people use the mass media and channels of communication, how nations can understand one another, how society can use mass media to its greatest good, and in general, how the basic process of communication work....Research on relative effectiveness of different media of communication include (i) what role the media play for the people (ii) how they motivate the people to bring about a change in their value orientation and perception (iii) which media are relatively more effective."[1]

It is not only difficult but almost impossible to come out accurately with the facts and figures about the impact of a mass media on the society, particularly in India, because "social sciences and their research methodology are very young in India and other Asian countries."[2] So far the scope of this study is concerned, Western style of surveys and social studies can be partly useful. The total surveys involve a huge machinery and can only be conducted by the institutions equivalent to Census department.

So far the communication research is concerned, it will be appropriate to quote Elihu Katz, the well-known communication researcher and teacher who told the BBC audience: "The researchers are convinced rightly I would say, there is no use just studying audiences; one must have access to producers and contents as well." According to him, "the broadcasters are interested in their audience is not as self-evident as it sounds." In U.L. Baruah words, "It is said professionalisation of broadcasting have meant increasing importance of peer judgements rather approval of clients. Having asked the audience what is wanted the professionals have 'discovered' that it always wanted the wrong thing". According to him, communication research is stimulated by:

— competitiveness of broadcasting.

— professional concern with service and with responsibility.

— need for a reliable source of evaluation of performance and allegations of departure from rule as a preferred method of accountability.

— desire to cope with challenges to receive professional practice.

— interest in identifying and improving organisational conditions, which are conducive to creativity.

Hence Communication researchers today want to study not only audiences and contents, but also the Producer, his working environment, and values, the tacit assumptions and paradigms that guide broadcasters in their decisions, alongwith a systematic monitoring of content for balance and possible bias. Simultaneously, there is need to refine methods of sociological research to measure the actual quantum of listening and viewing and their impact on society."[3]

In the field of social science, the studies and research work has been mostly to find-out the impact and influence of the various methods of mass communication on the Socio-Economic developments which is commonly measured in SES terms (Socio-Economic-Status), and the conclusions are derived on the basis of 'samples' collected from the different regions. The interest and affection to the music and art and change or reinforcement in values is different from other social studies and rather difficult, because of the deep rooted cultural values in India. Just because of this reason, our art forms are alive, after facing so many political and social disturbances.

The main objective of this study is to approximately workout the total exposure of the broadcasting, its reliance and influence on the society, its power and potential to motivate the people to bring about a change in the cultural values, and how the people of other nations are influenced by the culture and traditions of our country, particularly in the field of Hindustani Music.

It is appropriate to mention here that exposure to the media and the reliance on the media are two different phenomenon which may or may not be co-related. "Reliance indicate the opinion of the people about credibility of various media, where as exposure referes to the reception of information through media. A person may be more exposed to some particular media but may not put reliance on them."[4]

The study of co-relation and relative effectiveness is also not much important in this case, as in the case of SES surveys. In the case of music traditions 'Sound' is the only medium which is important, and study is concerned only about the total exposure and impact of 'Sound Medium' i.e. radio. There is no comparison with the print media, telephone, transport etc. which are hardly useful in this case. However, the role of Television has been included in this study, comparatively.

The study includes:

(i) Total exposure in terms of hardware components like number of transmitters, population and area covered.

(ii) Progress in software like broadcast of music programmes in terms of quality and quantity, its percentage and total hours of broadcast, and the programme policy in general.

(iii) Reliance and influence—The reports of different surveys conducted in this regard, analysis of impact on society, and influence on the performing artists and their status.

(iv) Co-relation—Impact of the other media suited for music programmes, i.e. television and its relative effectiveness.

(v) The scope of future progress in this field.

The facts, figures, analysis and conclusions in this work are mentioned on the basis of the material available. However, there is much more scope to study the impact of broadcasting on Hindustani Music, and this study is prelude to all such studies which will be conducted in future.

References

1. S.C. Sharma, *Media Communication and Development*, p. 76.
2. *Ibid.*
3. From U.L.Baruah, *This is All India Radio*, pp. 188-189.
4. S.C. Sharma, *Media Communication and Development*, p. 78.

4

Expansion of Music Items after Independence

It is evident from the earlier history of broadcasting in India that there was no stated policy for the broadcasting of music programmes till the end of fifties. The policy which came during the period of Sardar Patel, was, on the contrary, an attack over the music programmes which stated that "persons whose private life was public scandal should not be allowed to broadcast. This was evidently an attack on the dancing and singing girls and their more notorious sisters and professional musicians, and was, in effect, an expression of the puritan streak in governmental thinking."[1] Most of the performing artists in the north were dancing and singing girls and their Ustads, who were banned over radio. If fact, these Baijis were the preservers of our traditional art. In the absence of state patronage, dancing and singing became their profession which was not respected in the society. "It was their public life which was not considered respectable". Wrote Mr. Awasthy, "However the effect of this order was temporary and soon Baijis acquired respectability and allowed to broadcast as 'Devis".[2] So far as the programme planning is concerned, old trend of booking the artists for music programmes continued till the assumption of office by Dr. Keskar as Minister of Information and Broadcasting, in 1952.

Policy Directive and Audition System

The Keskar's period is said to be the Golden period in the history of AIR, so far as the classical music programmes are concerned. During this period (1952-61) not only a conscious policy came in to existence, but the music programmes over the radio were improved in quality and quantity both. Audition system for the purpose of selecting the artists came into existence and duration of classical music programmes was considerably increased. Dr.Keskar was himself a pioneer of Hindustani music and took keen interest in improving the quality of radio programmes. "The biggest impact on Indian music over the Radio was however, felt only in the years (1952-61) when Dr. Keskar was Minister for I&B, the longest tenure of any minister, before or after. He was keenly interested in and knowledgeable about Hindustani classical music and took several steps with the intention of improving its range and quality and encouraging musicians in the category."[3] Stated Mr. Awasthy, "Dr. Keskar was fortunate in being at the helm of affairs for ten years and thus able not only to put his policies into practice but also to see the results."[4]

Major achievements during the tenure of Dr. Keskar are as follows:

(a) New Audition System.
(b) Popularising classical music.
(c) National programme of Music.
(d) National Orchestra—Vadya Vrind.
(e) Annual Radio Sangeet Sammelan.
(f) Production of light music and processing of records by the Transcription Service.
(g) Vividh Bharati Service for light music listeners, and Programme Exchange Unit.[5]

New Audition System—Constitution of Audition Board

Under the new system, two Audition Boards for North and South Indian music were setup for systematic grading of the artists. Fee of the artist was decided according to the merit and grade. "The Audition Board was itself described as the Jury and the Northern Panel was placed under the chairmanship of Pandit S.N. Ratanjankar."[6] The Jury insisted on every performing musician appearing in person and apart from listening to the artist, the jury often questioned them on points of theory. Differences between the Gharanas and various schools of Indian music are well known and accepted throughout the country and these add no doubt to the richness of the classical tradition. The jury system, however, led to the impression among artists that a set of persons were out to foist the views of one Gharana on all the others."[7]

Many more problems arose when the top grade artists were not exempted from audition. "At many stations, Artists' Association were formed to fight new system. While musicians at smaller centres were forced to appear or were debarred from broadcasting, the initial auditions could not be carried-out either in Calcutta or Bombay. After prolonged negotiations in 1953-54, a large number of artists at Calcutta were 'exempted' from appearing in person before the jury. On the recommendations of the Station Directors, they were fitted into new grades in such a way that their existing fees remained untouched."[8]

Considering these objections and protests, new provisions were incorporated in the revised rules. "The description of the Board as the Music Jury, was substituted by the title 'The Music Audition Board.' Provision was made for exempting well- known artists from appearing before the Board. The Audition Board are now required to assess the quality of a performance as a piece of listening and are prohibited from putting questions to the artist. Roll numbers have been introduced and members of the Board do not see the artist. And finally a member of the staff is present at each audition as an observer."[9]

The Music Audition Board was unable to deal with the large number of artists from all over the country. The artist sometimes had to wait for two to three years to qualify the audition. To meet this difficulty, Local Audition Committees were set-up at each station to decentralise the work. In the case of light music, Local Audition Committee is empowered to approve the artist for broadcast. In the case of classical music, recordings are sent to MAB after initial screening by Local Audition Committee. The artist is allowed to broadcast only after the approval of MAB. The artists are graded by MAB as Top-ranking, 'A','B-High', and 'B' and fee of the artist is fixed accordingly. The artist is required to reappear before the MAB for upgrading.

The system continued till date and worked well and said to be the better than earlier systems. The merits and demerits of the system will be discussed in detail in the chapter 7.

Popularising Classical Music

In 1952-53 when a slogan *'Popularising Classical Music'* went around, almost every station, without assessing the available talent, taste of the listener and regional diversities, started broadcasting classical music for long hours replacing light and film music. The stations were asked to report periodically on their progress in this regard. Moreover, stations were also asked to broadcast classical music of the other regions. For example, North Indian stations were asked to broadcast South Indian music and vice versa. Number of stations started music lesson programmes to educate the listener about classical music. In addition to the originated programmes of classical music, stations were also asked to relay National Programmes of Music for 90 minutes on each Saturday from 9-30p.m. to 11p.m. from Delhi. The film music was regarded as vulgar and cheap. The broadcast of film music, if not stopped completely, its duration was considerably reduced. With the result, most of the listeners started tuning to Radio Ceylon for their entertainment, and the listening of AIR was considerably reduced, which was proved by a survey conducted in 1955.[10]

"Any quantitative increase is not always the best method of popularising an art form"[11] wrote Mr. Awasthy......Although, this was the most ambitious approach to popularise classical music, the overdose, all of a sudden, met with adverse results. The quantity of the classical music should have been increased slowly and day by day, after periodical monitoring the reactions of the listeners in a planned manner. However, in later years, the ratio of classical and light music was properly adjusted by opening a separate channel for light listeners, i.e., Vividh Bharati.

National Programme of Music

The concept of the 'National Music' was first conceived by Pt.V.N. Bhatkhande, in his presidential address to the All India Music Conference, held in Baroda in 1916:

"I feel happy at the thought that I have been able to mould a model for my successors to improve upon and to perfect, and

I cannot but hope that in a few years more, there will be an easy system for the instructions of our music, which will lead itself of mass education. Then will the ambition of India be fulfilled, for then the Indians will be common and universal. And if it please providence to so dispense that there is a fusion between the two systems of the North and South, then there will be a *'National Music'* for the whole country and the last of our ambitions will be reached, for then the great Nation will sing one song."[12]

The concept of Pt.Bhatkhande was first materialised by All India Radio in 1952, when on 20th July, first weekly programme of National Music for 90 minutes duration was broadcast from Delhi station and relayed by all stations of AIR, featuring Pt. Ravi Shanker, a well-known great master of Sitar. In this programme distinguished artists of both, Hindustani and Karnatak music have given their performances, irrespective of school or Gharana. Prior to that a 30 minutes programme entitled 'Music of India' was broadcast from Delhi which was also relayed by all stations of AIR. National Music replaced this programme of 20th July, 1952.[13]

This was the greatest landmark in the history of broadcasting in India, so far the classical music programmes are concerned. The listeners were first introduced to some of the best artists of Hindustani and Karnatak music, in a boarder way. Since then, the programme is continuing till date and number of great artists of India have so far been heard through this programme. Since the programme is relayed by all stations of AIR, almost, every corner of the country is covered and this programme is heard even out-side India. The programme is presented with special care introducing the artist his Gharana and stylish pecularities etc.

"It is well known that for this programme the choice of the artist could not be finalised without the approval of the Minister. Even a minor change in the date on which a particular artist was to appear had to be referred to him. (This was a rigid procedure during Dr. Keskar regime). The future of any programme lied in its being rescued from the personal domain of any one person. Unless the normal procedure of programme planning are applied to it there can be no hope of improvement.

In the first place certain definite criteria must be laid down for the selection of the artist of this programme."[14]

However, at the later stages, situation improved and National programme has maintained its standard. At present National programme is featuring (i) Prerecorded programmes in the studios (ii) Recordings of classical concerts before the invited audience and (iii) Programmes recorded at various stations in the case of regional and zonal artists.

National Orchestra

The AIR Vadya Vrind (National Orchestra) was formed in 1952 itself at Delhi station with 27 instruments. Hindustani compositions were looked after by Pt. Ravi Shanker while composings of Karnatak music were supervised by T.K. Jayarama Iyer. After Pt. Ravishanker left AIR, Late Shri Pannalal Ghose, a well-known flute artist tookover. This was the first attempt on the national level to broadcast harmonical compositions using the notations system of Indian Music. Although the attempt was appreciated by most of the artists in the country, this could not be continued for long and after Pt. Ravishanker, T.K. Jayarama Iyer, Yemni Shanker Shastry, Pannalal Ghose, Timir Baran, no further attempts were made to produce new compositions as the listeners' response was poor. Attempts were also made earlier by AIR stations to produce such harmonical compositions but not at the National level in such an organised way. For example, at the Lahore station under the direction of Jeevan Lal Mattoo, useful work was done during 1945-47. Similarly D.Amel has a lot of good work to his credit carried out at Bombay station. The initial step to setup an AIR Orchestra was taken up in 1949. The Karnatak wing was created in 1951. Even after the creation of National Orchestra in 1952, number of other stations produced good orchestral compositions by using instrumentalists on its staff.[15]

However, these compositions, western in nature, could not please Indian ear, since the Indian music has melody as its base. The compositions were also not purely harmonical in nature as the rules of harmonical compositions were not strictly followed playing different cords simultaneously by different instruments or groups. In fact, in Indian orchestra, it was the same chord, repeated and followed by all the instrumentalists. This was the experiment, first of its kind in the history of Indian classical music.

Radio Sangeet Sammelan

On 27th February, 1953, a note to Director General of All India Radio was sent by the Minister of I&B Dr. Keskar, stating, "In the North, there is nothing analogous to the Music academy like the one in existence in the South. It might be advantageous for us to establish such an institution in the North which will serve the combined purpose of music conferences, music festivals and music competitions. With the purpose and guidance of All India Radio, such a conference and competition is bound to assume important and become a regular feature. The time of the Dussehra and Diwali festivals appears to me to be the most appropriate."[16] Station Directors, Madras and Calcutta commented that they are not in favour of organising such conferences, as Madras station was already covering annual music festivals organised by three prominent local 'Sabhas' in addition to the Tyagaraja Festivals.

However, efforts continued and according to Mr.Luthra: "The Radio Sangeet Sammelan was started in 1955"[17] But according to Mr. Awasthy: "The first Radio Sangeet Sammelan concert was broadcast on 23rd October, 1954. It can be aptly called the Annual Music Meet."[18] The date referred by Mr. Awasthy seems to be correct as the I&B Minister in his note desired to broadcast it during Dushehra-Diwali festivals.

The duration of the classical music at the national level was thus increased considerably. Every year, music concerts were arranged and masters of the Hindustani and Karnatak music invited in these concerts to perform before the invited audience. These concerts were spread over a week at various auditoriums and recordings of these concerts are broadcast from Delhi station and relayed by all stations of AIR. On Sundays, an additional morning session is broadcast. These sessions are broadcast throughout the month. Earlier, the duration of each concert was for two hours (from 10p.m. to midnight). Nowadays the duration of each concert has been reduced to one hour except on Saturdays, where the duration is 90 minutes.

The most important aspect of these conferences was to bring two schools of music closer. The artists and listeners of the two varieties can better understand the stylistic peculiarities of each other's art. Radio Sangeet Sammelan, in fact provided a common platform to the musicians and scholars of both the schools and brought them closer. Inaugurating the 1959, Radio Sangeet Sammelan (Oct. 24) the President, Dr. Rajendra Prasad expressed: "It has given considerable encouragement not only to masters of the art, but also to young rising musicians. As a result of these annual competitions, Karnatak and Hindustani styles of music tended to come closer and there has been appreciable increase in the number of those who are about to understand and enjoy music of both types."[19]

In the first instance, there were sharp reactions shown by the listeners and even by the producers and artists of the other programmes. These broadcast, by them, regarded as 'overdoses' of the classical music. The reactions were quite natural. In those days, the percentage of listeners of classical music was very much small as compared to other light and film music. Reacted Shri Awasthy:

"There are so many music conferences every year in various cities of India where for days together marathon sessions of music are held and thousands attend, but what useful purpose does AIR seeks to serve by giving a glut of classical music during a particular period? Do these overdoses make classical music popular? Can even the genuinely interested listeners find so much time to tune in? And what is the fate of those whose first love is not classical music? Characteristically enough, the authorities have avoided any research on the listening commanded by the Sangeet Sammelan or for that matter by any other important programme."[20]

However, the annual concerts of Radio Sangeet Sammelan have played an effective role in popularising classical music through Radio. This has been proved in the listeners' survey reports which will be discussed in the following chapters. The effectiveness of radio is itself enough to popularise any art form wrote Mr. Ahuja, which is true to classical music also: "Radio, and television not only effect many of the elements in our society's every day life, but also exert a direct influence on the individual listener and on listeners collectively. This influence must be considerable if only because of the number of individuals reached and the amount of time during which they are exposed to radio or television."[21]

Radio Weeks Celebrations

Around 1956-57, a tradition of celebrating 'Radio Weeks' at different regional stations, was also started in which prominent artists of the region were invited to perform before the invited audience. These concerts were broadcast directly from the concert halls. In such a programme, our pioneer like Ustad Allauddin Khan Saheb was invited at Bhopal. However, with the introduction of Radio Sangeet Sammelan at National level, these celebrations were discontinued.[22]

Regional Music Concerts

In addition to these national concerts, regional stations are now arranging regional studio concerts which are broadcast on third Friday of the month from 10p.m. to 11p.m. The programme is put out on 'State Hookup' and prominent artists of 'A' and B-High grade are invited to perform. This programme is relayed by all stations of the state.

Vividh Bharati

History of the music programmes in AIR will be incomplete without a detailed study of Vividh Bharati programmes which are the most popular service of All India Radio. It is unique in itself and is widely listened, not only in India but also in the other countries of the world. The birth of Vividh Bharati has its own history. In 1952, when the slogan 'Popularising Classical Music' went around, the film music was described as cheap and vulgar. Even before Dr. Keskar, this matter caused concern to AIR and efforts were made to substitute film music by good light music produced by AIR itself, but the efforts failed to replace film music. Dr. Keskar, in his enthusiasm to popularise classical music, banned film music from AIR almost completely. "Keskar has less patience with film songs and soon after he took over he decided that film songs were to form not more than 10% of the recorded music at any station to begin with (15% in exceptional cases.) This target was to be achieved within six months and total elimination of film songs in 18 months. The instructions about elimination of film songs were not to be applied at this stage to music of a religious character or to folk songs which might have been used in films. Further, officially it was always stated that there was no ban of film music in AIR, circumstances, however, led towards it. Anyway, broadcast of film music was drastically reduced."[23]

It was also decided to substitute film music by good quality of light music produced by AIR. This decision was taken in a hurry without making any assessment whether AIR is fully equipped to fulfil the requirement of the decision. It was decided that "the lyrics composed for AIR's light music would be of a high literary and moral quality and these would be set to tunes based on Ragas or folk songs and would avoid the influence of Western Jazz, so prevalent in film music. AIR had, however, no resource for the production of light music. The stations were hastily ordered to setup light music production units, and to some how fill the gap."[24]

Similar account is given by Shri Luthra: "To popularise light music, other than film music, stations were asked to produce good light music by offering prizes for good songs and compositions and to have selected ones processed by record manufacturing companies. For this purpose Light Music Production Units were setup, to begin with, at Delhi, Bombay, Allahabad, Calcutta, Madras, Ahmedabad and Vijaywada, but their output was not generally of a high quality and they failed to take the place of film songs in listeners' preferences."[25]

This was the most unsuccessful attempt. The banning of film music, considerably reduced the listening of AIR stations and listeners defected to Radio Cylon, where broadcast of film songs and commercials was stepped up. On the other hand, film producers were also not very happy with AIR and few of them had refused to permit the broadcast of their songs from AIR.

The situation created, was never anticipated by the authorities, and Govt. started manipulating in this regard: "The tangle with film producers took several years to settle. It was stated that there was no wholesale condemnation of film music and that AIR merely reserved the right to select what particular film songs it proposed to broadcast. The public was given impression that the film producers were really to blame in so far as they had not renewed their agreement with AIR."[26]

However, the policy was again reviewed in the light of the new situation arose, fresh agreements were signed with the film producers and popular film music programmes which were stopped earlier, came again on the air. Screening committees were setup for screening the film songs before broadcast. The delay by screening committees caused another problem. "The committees started by trying to screen old songs, many of which had been forgotten and were hardly in circulation. A new song had little chance of being broadcast while it was still popular. However, enlightenment came in due course, and film songs came to be broadcast fairly soon after their release."[27]

On the other hand, production of light music by AIR also continued. The main problem in the production of light music was to find out new producers and composers. "The professed light music producers in the film world stood already condemned. AIR, therefore, turned mainly to two classes of persons. Classical musicians, who were prepared to try out this new assignment, and lyric writers. It is interesting that persons like D.T. Joshi, the well-known Sitar player, and pupil of Inayat Khan, V.G. Jog, the violinist then a teacher at the Morris College, Lucknow, Gyan Prakash Ghose of Calcutta joined AIR's newly opened light music units. Among literary men may be mentioned Bhagwati Charan Verma in Delhi."[28]

The light music units could not deliver the goods as expected. Wrote Mr. Awasthy: "....no production with any pretence of any artistic excellence can be done as easily and quickly to order as the authorities supposed."[29] AIR managed with the producers and artists who were unsuccessful in films, but their voices could not sustain without proper orchestral accompaniment. In Bombay particularly unsuccessful artists of the film world find ready acceptance to AIR. "The result was that every thing that AIR had sought to avoid came back in the form of diluted replicas of what the film gave. Doubtless nothing particularly vulgar is turned out by AIR's light music units, but on the other hand neither has it succeeded in producing any tune of his own, and the popularity of the 'cheapest' of film music continues to thrive."[30]

The simple fact which was not taken into consideration by the authorities was the factor of remuneration. AIR tried to compete with the film industry where the remunerations paid to the artists are highest. The impact of the new policy of AIR effected the listening adversely, "A listeners' research conducted in order to assess the popularity of AIR broadcasts revealed that nine, out of ten houses in every street were found invariably to be tuned to Ceylon, and the receiver in the tenth house, was either out of order or out of commission. These findings were unpleasant enough to get the authorities thinking. Frantic efforts were made at the diplomatic level to stop Radio Ceylon (Now Sri Lanka) from undoing the Good Samaritan work, AIR was supposed to be doing. When Government of Ceylon refused to be dictated to, it was announced in Parliament on one glorious morning, that Radio Ceylon was popular only with teenagers, or with people whose tastes were at best adolescent."[31]

Mr. Awasthy further stated: "Instead of the obvious conclusion a very wrong one had been drawn. Administrative reasoning in democracy could not have been more dishonest."[32]

However, authorities started thinking that a service to fulfil the requirement of the light listeners, was necessary to compete with the popularity of Radio Ceylon. "While, for reasons of ego and prestige, the policies of AIR remained unchanged on paper, by way of concession to the taste of those sections of the population who were addicted to the cheap attractions of Radio Ceylon, it was decided to setup a new service known as the *All India Variety Programme*, that is, *Vividh Bharati*."[33] As per Mr. Luthra: "The All India Variety Programme (AIVP) more popularly known as 'Vividh Bharati' was introduced on October, 3, 1957 consisted mainly of film songs and it brought back with a vengeance what need not have been banned in the first instance."[34] Two high power transmitters (100 KW SW) each at Bombay and Madras were setup to cover whole country. Emphasis was given mainly to the light music variety programmes.

With the introduction of Vividh Bharati service, new chapter was opened in the history of AIR. Initially the duration of Vividh Bharati programmes was only for 5 hours on week days and 7.30 hours on Sundays and principal holidays. The duration of Vividh Bharati programmes was considerably increased almost immediately taking in view the taste and demand of the listeners. Since October, 2, 1963, the service was available for 11.15 hours on week days and 11.45 hours on Saturdays and 12.30 hours on Sundays. This expansion took place in eight intermediate stages when an increase of an hour or so was effected in the programmes on week days, Sundays and holidays. At present, total duration of Vividh Bharati programmes, on week days is 12 hours 15 minutes and on Sundays and holidays, it is 13 hours and 20 minutes.[35]

Programmes of Vividh Bharati are scheduled and prepared at its Bombay unit. Within a year of inauguration, it was felt that Vividh Bharati could be run better from Delhi and the office was shifted to the capital. Vividh Bharati, the Programme Exchange Unit and the Transcription Service the distinct, unrelated units were clubbed together in 1958 to form the office of the Director of Transcription and Programme Exchange Service. In later years, the Vividh Bharati unit was again transferred to Bombay as an independent unit.[36]

Vividh Bharati on Medium Wave

Originally, Vividh Bharati service was broadcast over two high power shortwave transmitters at Bombay and Madras. Though, two short wave transmitters covered almost entire country, reception in several parts was not satisfactory. Moreover, possession of short wave receiver was still beyond the pocket of common man. Taking in view these problems, it was found essential to put this service through medium wave, and it was proposed to install 23 low power medium wave transmitters. By 1962, 17 such transmitters were setup. At present there are 30 low power medium wave transmitters projecting Vividh Bharati programmes out of which 29 centres are converted into commercial service. The programmes are still prepared at Bombay and copies are dubbed and circulated to all the centres for broadcast. Stations are also contributing their good programmes to Vividh Bharati, regularly.[37]

Programme Composition of Vividh Bharati

"....the core of the programmes is light music and the marrow of light music in any case, in India is film music,"[38] wrote Shri Awasthy. The sole purpose behind starting a service like Vividh Bharati was to win back the listeners from Radio Ceylon. And for this purpose, it became essential to use film music. "It will be seen that over 60 percent of the programmes are based on gramophone records of film songs. There are not less than 3 daily request programmes with the usual paraphernalia of names and messages. There are seven non-request film song programmes per week, not to mention song stories and broadcast of film sound tracks on alternate Sundays."[39]

In addition to film music programmes, there are other varieties of music programmes like devotional, non-film light music (commercial records), folk music and AIR light music (Akashvani Sugam Sangeet produced by AIR). Karnatak session starts from 3.45p.m. which is again light and film music from South. There was a fifteen minutes daily programme of light instrumental music presented under the title Jhankar.

Classical Music from Vividh Bharati

Vividh Bharati also broadcasts, classical music programmes at least for one hour daily, out of which ten minutes are devoted to music lesson programme 'Sangeet Sarita', which is the experiment of its own kind to pupularise classical music among common men.

Other programmes

As mentioned earlier, Vividh Bharati programmes are not wholly music programmes, there are few spoken word programmes like humorous plays, interviews, talks etc. out of them 'Hawa Mahal' is the most popular programme. The formats of the programmes have changed several times since its inception. Several programmes have been dropped and new programmes were substituted taking in view the listeners' demand.

At present the composition of the programmes of different variety is as under:-[40]

Film music	51%
Light music	4%
Devotional music	5.5%
Folk music	5%
Classical music	7%
Spokenword progs. including news relays etc.	27.5%

Popularity of Vividh Bharati

A study of the survey reports on Vividh Bharati programmes would show that the programmes made an immediate impact on the audience. The instant impact on the listeners was that the audience which was defected to Radio Ceylon diverted to

AIR programmes. If we go through the survey reports on the different programmes of VB, it is proved beyond doubt, that few programmes have record listening. There are number of factors responsible for the rapid increase in listening of VB programmes:

(i) Suiting to the taste of light listeners

Taking in view the different social factors, the major part of the population has developed a taste for film music. In other words, 80% of our listeners are light listeners. Classical music and other literary programmes are beyond their capacity to understand and hence opening of VB service was a gift to them. If we consider this popularity, from the democratic point of view, we could not ignore the likings and dislikings of the majority.

(ii) Easily available on the bands of radio set

Radio Ceylon was available only on the Short wave bands and it was essential to the listener to own a short-wave set, which was beyond the approach of the general public. But VB service is now available on 30 low power medium wave stations in the country in addition to two high power short wave transmitters, it bacame easy for the poor listener to monitor the service on MW set. Thanks to the introduction of transistors, VB programmes are now within the reach of all kinds of listeners, like Pan and tea stalls, shoes shops, bullock carts and even paddle ricksha etc.

(iii) Composition of programme

This is one of the most important factor, responsible to increase the popularity of VB. Some 70% of the programmes are music programmes suiting the taste of listeners. With the introduction of education through music and humour, VB has played a vital role not only in providing variety and light entertainment, but also in improving the taste of audience.

Overall Popularity of Vividh Bharati Programmes

There cannot be any dispute over the mass popularity of VB programmes. The programmes are not only popular in India, but also listened to in neighbouring countries, South East Asia and Africa. The success of VB programmes can be assessed from the following references:

"1. If listeners' letters are any indication of the success of a programme then it might safely be stated that listeners have taken kindly to Vividh Bharati which tries to provide entertainment with Capital E....on an average three lakhs letters are received by Vividh Bharati every year."[41]

"2. Vividh Bharati has had over eleven lakh letters from the listeners so far. On an average, three lakh letters are received by Vividh Bharati every year."[42]

"3. Vividh Bharati is extremely popular both in India and neighbouring countries and on an average we get three lakh letters a year, a considerable number of them being from South East Asia and Africa."[43]

This was estimated in 1961-64. During the next ten to fifteen years, the listening of VB has increased many fold.

Listening of Vividh Bharati

Listening figures of Vividh Bharati programmes are more than satisfactory which can be verified from the survey reports of 1980. In four metropolitan cities 41 to 79 percent of the listeners are tuned to VB for all the seven days in the week. 12 to 23% are exposed to 3 to 5 days, 4 to 20% for one or two days, and listener, who never listen VB programmes is merely one out of hundred.[44]

Similarly, listening of classical music programmes broadcast from VB is also satisfactory. The listening of Sangeet Sarita programme is around 20%, Swar Sudha-5% and Anuranjini about 1%.[45]

Folk Music Programmes of AIR

Folk music and folklore is the basis of culture of any society and so is the case in India. Therefore, one cannot think of existense of AIR without folk music programmes. In order to achieve this end various methods were adopted, i.e., by inviting folk singers to the studios and spoting by sending out OB vans fitted with recording equipment to rural areas. With the introduction of tape recording in 1953, it became easier to record and preserve the rare folk and tribal music of which there is no dearth in the country. AIR has done considerable recordings of folk music in different dialects and these songs are occasionally exchanged by the stations and Programme Exchange Service. Few good folk songs were also processed by the Transcription Service enriching AIR's archive.

Light Music

The Light Music Units which were constituted to compete with film music were not successful as stated earlier. However, solo singing and Choral groups are popular at various stations and singers of the zone of the stations are very much given chance to sing over the radio. These singers and artists are auditioned by the Local Audition Committees formed at various stations and local talent is exposed to the listeners. Number of great light music artists and playback singers were first introduced by AIR. Approximate time slot is also provided for light varieties of music like Geet, Gazals, Bhajans, Qawwali etc. Light music concerts are also arranged by various stations inviting artists of other zones, periodically. These efforts have produced a number of good artists, like Shanta Saxena, Surinder Kaur, Asa Singh Mastana, Sandhya Mukerjee and so on.

References

1. H.R. Luthra, *Indian Broadcasting*, p. 305.
2. G.C. Awasthy, *Broadcasting in India*, p. 39.
3. H.R. Luthra, *Indian Broadcasting*, p. 305.
4. G.C. Awasthy's *Broadcasting in India*, pp. 40-41.
5. *Ibid.*
6. *Ibid.*
7. *Ibid.*
8. *Ibid.*
9. *Ibid.*
10. *Ibid.*, pp. 41-44.
11. *Ibid.*, p. 43.
12. Pt. V.N. Bhatkhande, *A Short Historical Survey of the Music of Upper India*, p. 50.
13. G.C. Awasthy, *Broadcasting in India*, pp. 45-47.
14. *Ibid.*, p. 46.
15. *Ibid.*, pp. 44-50.
16. H.R. Luthra, *Indian Broadcasting*, p. 312.
17. *Ibid.*
18. G.C. Awasthy, *Broadcasting in India*, p. 49.

19. *Ibid.* pp. 49-50.
20. *Ibid*
21. B.N. Ahuja, *Mass Communication*, p. 179.
22. From the record of AIR, Bhopal.
23. G.C. Awasthy, *Broadcasting in India*, p. 51.
24. *Ibid.*
25. H.R. Luthra, *Indian Broadcasting*, p. 309.
26. G.C. Awasthy, *Broadcasting in India*, pp. 51-52.
27. *Ibid.*
28. *Ibid.*
29. *Ibid.*, pp. 52 to 54.
30. *Ibid.*
31. *Ibid.*
32. H.R. Luthra, *Indian Broadcasting*, p. 310.
33. *Ibid.*, pp. 310-12.
34. *Ibid.*, p. 54.
35. H.R. Luthra, *Indian Broadcasting*, p. 310.
36. *Ibid.*, pp. 310-12.
37. G.C. Awasthy, *Broadcasting in India*, pp. 51-55, and H.R. Luthra's, *Indian Broadcasting*, p. 111.
38. *Ibid.*
39. G.C. Awasthy, *Broadcasting in India*, p. 53.
40. Calculated from Vividh Bharati Progs. Broadcast.
41. *Akashvani* (English) issue dated 1-10-1961.
42. *Ibid.*, dated 27-1-1963.
43. G.C. Awasthy, *Broadcasting in India*, quoting an article.
44. See tables 14 and 15 in the Appendix
45. *Ibid.*

5

Function of Archives and Programme Exchange

Transcription and Programme Exchange

Established in fifties, programme exchange service of All India Radio has played a tremendous role in the field of popularising music by entertaining and educating the different cultural groups of the country, by means of exchange of programmes. This is the best available system by means of which, programmes of one region can be listened in the other. The varieties of music and its artists, are scattered all over the country, and it is also essential to make the people conversant with different varieties of music, and programme exchange is the simplest way of doing so. It is practically difficult, if not impossible to invite all the artists of the country by any one station, which involves lot of expenditure on travelling etc. But the recordings done at one station can be sent to other saving huge amount of money and time. "All AIR stations are required to send to the Director of Transcription and Programme Exchange Service, recordings of music, talks, plays, features and other programmes which are of high quality and may be of interest of wider audiences than those commanded by the originating stations......The service issue a fortnightly bulletin to all stations listing the programmes available with short descriptive notes, from which the stations can choose items for rebroadcast. Royalty and other rebroadcast fees in accordance with the terms of the original programme contract, are payable by the stations which rebroadcast the programme."[1]

The service of programme exchange is useful in so many ways. Recordings of high quality programmes from all over the country are available for use by the stations willing to rebroadcast the programmes. On the other hand, small stations where recording facilities are not available, or the talent is not available in the area of the station, can get the ready made material from DTPES. Programmes like music, plays, features are available in Hindi, Urdu and English but large number of programmes available with the DTPES are *music programmes.* This enables the stations to broadcast the programmes and performances of the artists of other regions, which can be termed as cultural exchange.

Programme Exchange Service, also sends some important recordings of music and other featurised programmes to friendly countries, to be broadcast by the home services of such countries. This practice is popularising our culture and music in other European and American countries.

AIR Archives

Recordings of the old masters and national figures are preserved in AIR Archives. Today, we are in a position to listen the pioneering work of our old masters like Bade Gulam Ali Khan, Alla Uddin Khan, Abdul Karim Khan, D.V. Palusker and others. "At present consist of 26,700 tapes, scripts, other written material and photographs of great historical value. Recordings of the views of national figures such as Mahatma Gandhi, Ravindranath Tagore, Pt. Jawaharlal Nehru, Sardar Vallabh Bhai Patel, Netaji Subhash Chandra Bose, and Lord Mountbatten are available. Recordings by distinguished musicians and literary figures are also preserved in the archives."[2]

The library has a capacity of 30,000 tapes, and out of 26,700 tapes already available, 5502 contains *various music programmes.* A list of selected artists whose recordings are available is given in the table 18 (Appendix).

Old Masters

"The pride of AIR's collection is the recordings of music recitals by master musicians who are either no more or have passed their prime. Some of the artists who are no more and whose recordings are available include Abdul Karim Khan, Allauddin Khan, Amir Khan, Bade Gulam Ali Khan, Hirabai Barodekar, Begum Akhtar, Bundu Khan, T. Chowdiah, Faiyas Khan, Pannalal Ghose, Hafeez Ali Khan, Ariyakudi Ramanuja Iyengar, Madurai Mani Iyer, Musiri Subramania Iyer, Chambai Vaidyanatha Bhagwatar, Dwaram Venkataswamy Naidu, Mushtaq Hussian Khan, Onkarnath Thakur, D.V. Paluskar, Rajab Ali Khan, Rasoolan Bai, S.N. Ratanjanker, Shakoor Khan, etc."[3]

These programmes are very much useful on anniversaries and festivals also. Moreover, "AIR has released over fifty recitals by old masters to various gramophone companies, who have reproduced them on commercial discs available in the market,"[4] keeping in view the public interest. On special occasions, national and network programmes are based on the preserved recordings, and stations can indent material from Archives for their use.

In order to continue the process of enriching the Archives, stations has been instructed to suggest the names of the artists of their zone, whose recordings are to be preserved in this library, and usually, 90 minutes programme is recorded after paying 4 times of their normal fee. "Special efforts are now being made to aquire for archives voice-recordings of eminent Indians and music recitals by prominent artists when they are top of their form."[5]

A scheme for the purpose of increasing the capacity of the library from 30,000 to 50,000 tapes has been approved by the NLF committee in addition of listening and dubbing facilities.[6]

Since the availability of the INSET channels to AIR, important recordings are being fed to the stations through its R.N. Channels, which was introduced in 1987. Through this device, items can be recorded at a particular time simultaneously by all stations, from Delhi, further saving time and money in transportation of such material.

References

1. P.C. Chatterjee, *Broadcasting in India*, p. 80.

2. *Ibid.*
3. U.L. Baruah, *This is All India Radio*, p. 227.
4. P.C. Chatterjee, *Broadcasting in India*, p. 81.
5. U.L. Baruah, *This is All India Radio*, pp. 227-28.
6. *Ibid.*

6

Experimentation

VADYA VRIND AND OTHER ORCHESTRAL COMPOSITIONS EFFORTS AND PLANNING TO POPULARISE CLASSICAL MUSIC PROGRAMMES

Vadya Vrind and Other Orchestral Compositions

AIR, not only popularised Indian Classical music in its traditional form, but did innovative efforts to give new dimensions in this field. In fact, Indian music mostly represents melodic system where artist has got full scope to make free improvisations while performing. There is no place to harmony and other orchestral compositions where one composer composes the tune, which in turn is followed by a group of artists. Harmonical compositions, as said earlier is a Western concept, where an artist does not have any choice to play or sing according to his imaginations. However, this tradition entered in our country with the invasion of Europeans and became popular. After Independence when a policy of broadcasting music programmes was formulated, it was considered important to introduce orchestral compositions based on Indian Classical music.

During British period, such efforts were made to bring Indian and Western music closer. "Foulds was fascinated with the idea of introducing harmony into Indian music,"[1] wrote Luthra. Efforts were also made by few Indian musicians to compose orchestral music. The problem was that it does not suit to the Indian traditions and artists were not accustomed to play according to the notations. Group of artists, number of instruments, funds and long rehearsals were the other problems faced during those days. However, efforts continued till the formation of 'National Orchestra'.

The initial steps towards the setting up of an AIR Orchestra go back to the year 1949. The Vadya Vrind, however, came into existence in 1952, with 27 instruments. Its Hindustani section was under Pt. Ravishanker, later Late Pannalal Ghose looked after the section after Pt. Ravishanker left AIR. Karnatak Section was supervised by T.K. Jayaraman Iyer.

This was the first real step taken by AIR in experimentation in the history of broadcasting classical music. In orchestral compositions, it is very difficult to maintain the basic character of Indian music which is mainly based on imagination of the artist. "An orchestral composition normally meant an ensemble of a number of instruments playing in unison,"[2] wrote Awasthy. Similar views are of S.P. Jain, the writer of the *Art of Broadcasting*, according to him: "The orchestra does not offer any room for individual improvisation. It calls for absolute team spirit and discipline. The selection of an instrument or a group of instruments is to be made judiciously. In an Indian orchestra, the use of stringed bowed instruments is quite prominent, perhaps because it lends a kind of melodic fulness in the orchestral piece and it is the mainstay of an orchestra. The National Orchestra of AIR Vadya Vrind is perhaps the only Indian ensemble roughly comparable to Modern Western Chamber Music."[3]

Pt. Ravishanker, when he joined AIR as the Director of Music for the External Service Division, made such efforts. He was influenced by the Western compositions while he was travelling Europe with his elder brother. In his own words:"The early musical experiments I did when I was with Dada's troupe in Europe later had motivated me to try ballet music and film scores," he wrote in his autobiography, "and now I was determined to experiment further in compositions of a predominantly Indian nature that is, pieces that retained as much as possible the Indian character and the quality of Indian sound." In his earlier compositions, he used all Indian instruments—he mentioned: "the ensemble I worked which consisted of the sitar, veena, sarod, sarangi, Vichitra veena, flutes, jaltarang (China bowls of different sizes filled with water and played by sticks), tabla, dholak, and many other kinds of drums, cymbals and percussion instruments."[4]

It was a co-incident that Pt. Ravishanker got a field and a media to spread his ideas to the music loving people. With the formation of Vadya Vrind in AIR, Pt. Ravishanker was transferred to the Home service of AIR. "There, I was very pleased to be able to organise a larger ensembles that was known as Vadya Vrind, or National Orchestra, with which I continued to work for the next few years. This orchestra was very much like the instrumental ensemble I had been working with earlier, only it was considerably enlarged. In particular the string section had been greatly augmented and now included many Western instruments of the violin family."[5]

An artist who was devoted to Indian music and Indian instruments had changed his mind and adopted Western instruments:"In my childhood, so often had I heard, Uday refuse to use one single Western instrument in the troupe's orchestral ensemble that his adament and repeated refusal made a strong impression in my mind". Pt. Ravishanker wrote: "but as my musical senses matured, especially while I was with All India Radio, I slowly came to change my attitude and realized that Western instruments, especially violins and their relatives, could portray Indian music most beautifully and, in fact, had been used in India by outstanding musicians for many years."[6]

The experiment was possible because Pt. Ravishanker was free to work according to his ideas. He accepted: "I was completely free to utilize any instruments I chose, including Western instruments, that I used for special effects. I could take any style- and any forms of music and very freely work them into the compositions. Even if a classical raga was used at some point, I could leave it intact to sustain a mood or mix it with several other ragas in quick succession for another kind of effect."[7]

The Orchestral Music, is, purely the idea emerged from the organisation called All India Radio. The success of the experiment is another matter and could be discussed later. How much it was liked by the music loving people and whether the thematic compositions were really emitting the themes on which the compositions were derived? Howmuch it was understood or appreciated by the listeners? These questions to be considered separately. However, credit for this new experiment goes to All India Radio.

Music Lesson Programmes

The popularity of orchestral compositions, although it was a new experiment, was short lived and did not find favour with the listeners. However, another experiment to popularise classical music by AIR was most successful one, and that was Music lesson programme.

First step to popularise classical music was initiated in 1952-53 when stations were not only asked to increase the duration of the classical music programmes, but also were asked to report periodically. During this period, "a large number of stations introduced 'Music Lesson' programmes"[8] to educate listeners. The main objective behind broadcasting these programmes was to create interest and to produce listeners for classical music programmes broadcast from AIR, and to nullify the effect and popularity of Western music. These programmes gave some idea of classroom teaching and beginners were attracted. However, success of such programmes could only be gauged after few years.

I personally know something about these programmes broadcast from AIR stations. For example, Bhopal station has broadcast two programmes a week during 1971-74, named as Ranjana and Subaddha Sangeet, out of which one programme Subaddha Sangeet continued till 1988. I do not recall the name, but such programmes were broadcast earlier also. Similar efforts were made by other stations also. These efforts paid dividends and number of listeners responded to these programmes.

Vividh Bharati service is known for its light entertainment, but this service has played an effective role in popularising classical music through its experiment. When light and film music entertains larger amount of population, it was thought that any education given through light or film entertainment will bring the results, and light and film music can be used as a medium for education, and experiment carried-out by AIR was fruitful beyond expectation. It was found appropriate to broadcast short programmes of 'music lesson' based on popular film songs. Thanks to music directors with a classical background, who composed songs for films, based on classical ragas. These film songs were extremely popular among light music listeners, and the idea was to introduce classical music through film songs.

It is true that such programmes could not produce any artist. But the approach of such programmes was to develop new taste and to create an atmosphere where classical music would find its place in the society.

In addition to such programmes of 'Music lesson', Vividh Bharati service also started number of programmes based on film songs, composed on classical ragas, with suitable commentaries. Since these songs were the musical hits and extremely popular among the common public, an atmosphere was built up for listening of classical music programmes.

For example, in 1973, Vividh Bharati service introduced such a popular programme of music lesson named 'Sangeet Sarita' already discussed in earlier chapter. "The decline of popularity of classical music was something of great concern to the planners of Vividh Bharati. This in 1973, a new format for Vividh Bharati was introduced giving classical music a place of pride. The main concern to the planners was to revive this form of music. They tried to present classical music in its popular form like 'Sangeet Sarita', which introduced the listeners to various forms of 'ragas' and gave an opportunity to the listeners to compare them to the popular film songs based on those 'ragas'. This programme, incidentally, has become very popular with the listeners and is now in the eleventh year of its existence,"[9] wrote S.P. Jain in his *Art of Broadcasting* published in 1985. Now it is seventeenth year of its existence of this programme.

A series of programmes is suitably planned for a particular type of ragas. Introduction of raga is given in the beginning, mentioning its 'Jati', 'Thata' and notations etc. followed by the popular film song based on the raga. In the end, a piece of vocal or instrumental music is played, highlighting pure classical form of raga. The duration of the programme is for 10 minutes and time is 7-30 in the morning.

During the same period, another programme 'Swar Sudha' was introduced for 15 minutes in the evening. In this programme, vocal and instrumental pieces of a raga, sung or played by eminent artists are broadcast.

On Sundays, interviews from renowned artists and musicians are now broadcast in 'Sangeet Sarita' programme to enable the listeners to understand, how the great masters have achieved their goal, to which Gharana or school they belonged, and what are the qualities of their performances.

A fifteen minutes classical music programme was also introduced during the same period, scheduled at 3-30p.m. under the title 'Anuranjini'. Now the duration of this programme has been increased to 30 minutes. Once a week, request programme of classical music is broadcast in this programme, and listeners started responding to this, by sending their requests.

The total duration of classical music programmes broadcast from Vividh Bharati comes to 55 minutes daily. These efforts and experiments of Vividh Bharati planners were able to widen the taste of common listeners in the following years. So far the standard of these programmes is concerned, there is no doubt that Vividh Bharati is doing well.

In addition to the above classical music items, special programmes are also scheduled on a particular occassion like birth and death anniversaries of our great masters.

A weekly programme of light classical music has recently been introduced by Vividh Bharati under the title 'Swaranjali'. The duration is 15 minutes at 12-45p.m. on Sundays. Earlier, this programme was broadcast as 'Manjusha'.

Vividh Bharati programmes, through its short and medium wave transmitters are now reaching every remote corner of the country. The listening of these programmes is also un-questioned. No other programme of any other service in India has covered that much vast population. If the percentage figures of audience research are taken for assessment, it is revealed that several million people in India and abroad are regular listeners of these programmes. No school or college or any other cultural institution can reach, so easily and promptly to such a large amount of population, as this service has done. From our day to day experience, one fact is clear, that today, a society of music lovers and an audience for the classical music programmes has been created. Attendence in the concert halls is the best example.

What we observe today in the concerts of classical music, was not, in fact, visible a few decades ago.

It may, of course, be true that all the persons attending the concerts or listening to the classical music programmes are not well versed to understand or enjoy the programme. There may be several people who cannot even understand the basic qualities of the classical music, but they still listen and enjoy.

Earlier, such cultural activities were limited to big cities, but the cultural activities are now extended to small towns. It has become a culture now and intellectuals, business person, social workers, executives, officers and even political leaders are seen attending classical music concerts, and it has become a status symbol in the society. It is a different matter, how much they enjoy or understand.

A brief survey, through interviews has revealed that few of the listeners have really came to know the names and tunes of the raga through film songs broadcast in the music lesson and other classical music programmes.

It is true that such music lesson programmes, nor the music schools and colleges can produce any artist, for that, vigorous training under some established artist, Guru, or Ustad is essential. But at least, such programmes have successfully, created an atmosphere to understand our music. It is very difficult to say accurately, how many such listeners are motivated, but this can be said beyond doubt that such programmes have started cultural revolution, so far the popularity of Indian classical music is concerned.

Music Lesson Programmes by Regional Services

Since 1952, several regional stations also started such music lesson programmes. It was observed that short duration pieces of classical music (from 3 to 5 minutes duration) are extremely popular among light listeners. For this effect, artists were asked to conclude the raga within 5 minutes. It was, in the beginning, very difficult for the artist, who were habitual to sing or play for long hours. However, popularity on radio and efforts of AIR staff, convinced them to do so. At several stations, these cuts are broadcast even now under the title 'Kanhra ke Prakar' or 'Sarang ke Prakar' where a group of similar ragas is introduced. Few stations broadcast such items under the title 'Subaddh

Sangeet'. However, for various reasons, the broadcast of such programmes has been stopped at many stations.

References

1. H.R. Luthra, *Indian Broadcasting*, p. 303.
2. G.C. Awasthy, *Broadcasting in India*, p, 48.
3. S.P. Jain, *The Art of Broadcasting*, p. 27.
4. Pt. Ravishanker, *My Music My Life*, p. 82.
5. *Ibid.*
6. *Ibid.*, p. 83.
7. *Ibid.*
8. G.C. Awasthy, *Broadcasting in India*, p. 44.
9. S.P. Jain, *The Art of Broadcasting*, p. 33. Rest from the Schedule of Vividh Bharati Programmes.

7

Total Exposure and Impact

Total Exposure After Independence

In 1947, 'there were in all 14 Radio stations in the country, 9 controlled by All India Radio and other 5 by Princely States.'[1]

(a) Controlled by All India Radio:

- (i) Bombay
- (ii) Calcutta
- (iii) Delhi
- (iv) Madras
- (v) Tiruchirapalli
- (vi) Lahore
- (vii) Peshawar
- (viii) Dacca
- (ix) Lucknow

} After partition, Stations (vi)–(viii) were taken-over by Pakistan Govt.

(b) Controlled by Princely States:

- (i) Mysore
- (ii) Baroda
- (iii) Hyderabad
- (iv) Aurangabad
- (v) Trivendrum

With the integration of these states with Union of India, stations also became the part of AIR network. 'At that time only 9 percent of the population of the country was covered by AIR."[2]

The Ministry of Information and Broadcasting under the leadership of Sardar Vallabh Bhai Patel, decided to setup new stations in the country. "It was decided first to setup 'Pilot' stations in the various linguistic zones, and then to instal highpower transmitters at the regional and zonal stations."[3]

A radio station at Jullundhur was opened on 1st November, 1947 taking in view the situation in Panjab due to partition. Towards the end of the same year a critical situation arose in Kashmir and a radio station was setup by the State in Jammu on 1st December,1947. The year 1948 was marked by considerable extension of broadcasting facilities in various cultural zones of the country. Stations came-up during 1948 are:

Patna	26th Jan., 1948
Cuttuck	28th Jan., 1948
Amritsar	16th Feb., 1948
Shillong	1st July, 1948
Gauhati	1st July, 1948
Nagpur	16th July, 1948
Vijayawada	1st December, 1948
Baroda	Taken over by AIR on 16th Dec.,1948[4]

Planned Development

First Five Year Plan, 1951-56

Planned development of broadcasting was takenup only after implementation of first Five Year Plan in the year 1951.

During this period, broadcasting was not given much importance as it was considered as unproductive expenditure and not as an important activity for economic development which "is evident from the fact that broadcasting was not mentioned in the People's Edition of the First Five Year Plan brought out in January, 1953. It figured only in the appendix giving statistical tables under the head 'Transport and Communication.'"[5] And in all 3.52 crores were provided for the development of broadcasting.

Stations opened were Poona on 2nd Sep., 1953, (1KWMW) later replaced by 5 KW MW transmitter after one and a half year. Earlier stations at Srinagar and Jammu were run by the State Govt. were taken over by All India Radio on 13th April and 16th December, 1954 respectively. Other stations opened were Rajkot, Indore, Simla, Banglore and Ajmer in 1955.[6]

"Apart from the new stations opened, the First Plan saw the raising of strenght of several transmitters which enabled them to provide a stronger and more widely listened to signal in several regions."[7]

"The coverage at the end of First Five Year Plan had increased to 46 percent of the population."[8]

Important Programmes Introduced

National Programme of Music started on July 20, 1952 and other national programmes like talks on April 29, 1953, Operas, plays and features started in 1956 on July 14, 28th and August 14, respectively.[9]

The Second Five Year Plan 1956-61

Outlining the development programme of broadcasting in the country during Second Five Year Plan, the Planning Commission observed:

"The expansion which had taken place, during the First Plan ensures that each language has been provided with at least one transmitting station and that fairly effective coverage is available to almost all the regions. The aim during the Second Plan is to extend the services now available for all the languages to as wide as area as it is at present possible to reach. For areas in which terrain conditions are difficult short-wave transmitters are to be established. To meet the growing demands of national programmes and for ensuring country wide listening of national broadcasts, a 100 KW short-wave transmitter as well as a 100 KW medium wave transmitter will be setup at Delhi and 50 KW medium wave transmitter will be provided at Calcutta, Bombay and Madras. External Services will also be expanded."[10]

During the Second Plan, three new stations were commissioned, Bhopal in October, 1956, Tirichura on November 4, 1956 and Ranchi on July 27, 1957. "To improve the coverage of certain centres, 20 KW transmitters were provided at (i) Delhi on July 1, 1956 for the stations second channel (ii) Vijayawada on December 9, 1956 and (iii) Patna on December, 1959, to replace the old low power stations."[11]

In 1957 on October, 3, a new All India Variety Programme of Light Music, later called Vividh Bharati started. Two 100 KW short wave transmitters were commissioned at Bombay and Madras to radiate this programme.[12] The success of Vividh Bharati programmes has been discussed in earlier chapters.

During the Second Plan period, following centres were also started:-

(i) Chandigarh (Auxiliary Centre) on 09-04-1957.
(ii) Gauhati (10 KW MW) on 03-05-1957.
(iii) Delhi (100 KW MW) on 31-01-1960.

By the end of Second Plan coverage had increased to 55% of the population and area covered by 37% by medium wave.[13]

The Third Five Year Plan 1961-66

The Third Five Year Plan was mainly confined to extend the primary grade medium wave service as quickly as possible by adding a number of medium wave transmitters in network. 'The completion of Third Plan gave the primary service a coverage upto 70% of the population.'[14]

The growth of broadcasting during the Third Plan was maximum. During the period 22 new radio stations were installed and 2 auxiliary centres Shillong and Chandigarh were converted into full flegde broadcasting centres, and the total number of transmitters went upto 110 from 59 in 1961. The credit for fast expansion in the field of broadcasting goes to the then I & B Minister Dr. B.V. Keskar, who took personal interest in taking certain decisions. In order to bring out home service nearer to the listener, the need of extension of medium wave was very much felt. The Planning Commission has stated that "With the view to make the internal coverage more effective, provision is being made in the Third Five Year Plan to expand the medium wave broadcast service and to strengthen the arrangements for pre-recording of programmes. The Third Plan also includes provisions for further improvement of the external broadcast Services."[15]

The details were disclosed for the first time in 1960 by the Minister of Information and Broadcasting, Dr. B.V. Keskar, at a press conference. 'The Third Plan had been designed to double the number of transmitters in operating no less than fifty seven being added to sixty, the number at the time of formulation of the Plan.'[16]

Dr. Keskar explained the object of the Plan—the Medium Wave Plan as it is called:

"(a) To enable those areas and population groups to have programmes on medium wave channels, which are not at present within listening range of medium wave programmes.

(b) To encourage the production and use of low-cost radio sets, a single band medium wave set being cheaper to produce than an all-wave set.

(c) To provide an alternative light programme on medium wave (Vividh Bharati) and,

(d) To cover any other areas at present not satisfactorily served by AIR."[17]

Vivid Bharati (Expansion of coverage area)

Vividh Bharati programmes started on 3rd October, 1957 on two powerful shortwave transmitters at Bombay and Madras, part of these were relayed on Delhi(C) and some other stations for short intervals. Now Delhi(C) relays Vividh Bharati entirely except between 1945 and 2015 hours when it carried Urdu Majlis"[18]

Later under mediumwave plan during the period of Third Plan, Vividh Bharati service relayed by twenty-three additional one kilowatt medium wave transmitters scattered all over the country... At present Vividh Bharati service is relayed by 30 such transmitters out of which 29 are commercial centres.

Extension of Broadcasting in Remote Areas

From the beginning of the planned development in broadcasting, the question of opening radio stations in remote areas was given priority. "A special daily programme beamed to Andaman and Nicobar Islands was started from Delhi on Independence Day, August 1959. Much later, on June, 2,1963 these islands got their own station."[19]

After the Chinese aggression in October, 1962, Third Plan drawn up in 1960 was changed, considerably, because of the vaccum of broadcasting facilities was observed during the war time, "the priorities were therefore, revised. The projects, as actually completed in the Third Plan included a new station at Kurseong (June, 2, 1962) with a 2KW shortwave transmitter."[20] This was replaced by 20 KW shortwave transmitter after the Chinese attack.

Other stations opened during the period of Third Plan are: Kohima, Port Blair, Imphal, Pasighat and Bhuj. Bhuj Station covers 10 lakhs population in the district of Kutch (in Gujarat).

Goa station, which was setup by Portuguese colonial rulers was converted a station of All India Radio on January, 2, 1962."[21]

Auxiliary Centres

During the Third Plan period 22 Auxiliary centres were also commissioned, to relay the programmes from their respective regional stations. The centres are listed below:-

1. Bhopal	2. Ranchi	3. Varanasi	4. Rajkot
5. Gauhati	6. Bikaner	7. Srinagar	8. Sambalpur
9. Cuddapah	10. Siliguri	11. Vishakhapatnam	
12. Raipur	13. Sangli	14. Tirinuvelli	15. Jeypore
16. Gwalior	17. Jabalpur	18. Bhadrawati	19. Rampur
20. Jodhpur	21. Gulbarga	22. Shillong	

All mediumwave transmitters.[22]

At the end of Third Plan, total number of transmitters were 110, out of which 82 were medium wave and 28 shortwave transmitters. Total number of broadcasting centres 56 including 2 auxiliary recording centres. 26 Vividh Bharati centres were also installed during this period.

Since Independence, the progress was more than satisfactory as the number of broadcasting centres increased from 6 to 56 and number of transmitters from 18 to 110. The area covered by medium wave service was increased from 2.5% to 52% and population covered was raised from 11 to 70%.

Yearly Planning

The Fourth Five Year plan started on April, 1,1969. The period between the end of the Third Plan and beginning of Fourth Plan, i.e., from April 1,1966 to March, 31, 1969 was covered by annual planning. During this period of three years, five new stations and six auxiliary centres were commissioned. New stations opened were:-

(1) Aizwal -20 KW 31-7-66
(2) Mathura-1KW 29-1-67
(3) Pondicherry-1KW MW 23-9-67
(4) Tezu-250 watt-MW 15-8-67
(5) Dibrugarh-100 KW MW 2-2-69

Auxiliary centres, each with a 10 KW MW transmitters were setup at Coimbatore, Agartala, Udaipur, Bhagalpur, Suratgarh and Parbhani. These centres relayed the primary service of the existing stations in the area, and thus increased the programme coverage. These stations later became full fledged independent stations.

"With these installations, Akashvani's medium wave coverage as on March 31, 1969 was about 73% by population and 56% by area."[23]

Fourth Five Year Plan 1969-74

Important aspect of the Fourth Plan was the attention to the technical improvements. "The main emphasis at that time was laid on increasing the strength of the existing transmitters at stations and opening auxiliary centres such as those at Allepy (100 KW MW) on July, 1971 and Gorakhpur (10 KW MW) on October 2, 1972. A 1000 KW MW station was installed at Calcutta (September 22, 1969), 50 KW MW transmitters at Simla and Kohima on December 9, 1971 and November 14, 1972 respectively, Jammu a 50 KW MW transmitter in April 1970, and also high power medium wave transmitter at Jodhpur, Allepy and Imphal. In a further step to augment coverage to border areas a megawatt (1000 KW) medium wave transmitter was setup at Rajkot."[24] During this period, radiation power of several stations was also increased.

This plan witnessed two additional stations also. One was opened at Leh (10 KW MW) on 25-06-1971 which is in Jammu & Kashmir state and at present the highest installed transmitter in India and other station was Silchar (10 KW MW) on 11-08-71.[25]

"With this expansion, total population covered was about 80% and area covered was raised to 65.5%."[26]

Fifth Five Year Plan 1974-79[27]

The main objective during the Fifth Plan period was to improve the service in border areas and providing coverage on medium wave in remote areas which were not covered by medium wave service so far. Some eight new stations and four auxiliary stations were commissioned during this period.

New stations were opened at:-

1.	Tawang (in Arunachal Pradesh, being the 2nd highest in India)	23-09-1974
2.	Mysore 1 KW MW	14-11-1974
3.	Darbhanga 10 KW	02-02-1976
4.	Rohtak 20 KW	08-05-1976
5.	Chatterpur 20 KW	07-08-1976
6.	Aurangabad 1 KW	09-09-1976
7.	Ambikapur 20 KW	26-12-1976
8.	Jagdalpur 20 KW	22-01-1977

To improve the coverage of primary service following new auxiliary centres were also opened:-

1.	Jalgaon 20 KW	16-10-1976
2.	Brahmawar (Udipi) 20 KW	12-12-1976
3.	Ratnagiri 20 KW	03-01-1977
4.	Rewa 20 KW	02-10-1977

With the result on 31st March 1980, the coverage was increased by 89.40% by population and 77.75% by area."[28]

Under this Plan number of stations were shifted to new studio buildings which were started earlier in rented buildings with inadequate facilities.

It will be appropriate to mention here two most important achievements during this period. First, the T.V was separated from Radio on 1st April, 1976 and other was the introduction of FM (Frequency Modulation) system at Madras in July, 1977. Later FM facilities were also provided at Calcutta and Bombay.[29]

Sixth Plan

Approach of the planning was little different in the recommendation of the Planning Commission. "The four objectives of the Sixth Plan (1980-85) have been laid down as consolidation and expansion of regional service, strengthening of the External Services, development of a dedicated national broadcasting channel, and introduction of Local Broadcasting."[30]

Taking in view the cultural diversities and multiplicity of languages and dialects in the country, the concept of 'Local Radio' would have come much early. The only way to speak to the different cultural groups, Local Radio was the only alternative. "The Plan Document takes note of these factors and recognises that state boundaries do not conform to the range of its radio station. The fact that there is a radio station, nearby, does not help a listener unless it broadcasts in his own language and dialect and conforms to his cultural needs."[31]

Another problem arose due to the rapid growth of medium wave transmitters in other countries, was the interference in the night time to our regional service. This technical problem was considered in the International Telecommunication Union Conference held at Geneva in 1975. "The ITU allocations made it possible for Akashvani to initiate the process of setting up 352 low power transmitters of 1 KW each, all of these sharing three reserved frequencies and 428 medium and high power transmitters consisting of:-

1. One transmitter of 2 megawatt (2000 KW)
2. Five transmitters of 1 megawatt (1000 KW)
3. 177 transmitters of 300 KW each.
4. 15 transmitters of 200 KW each.
5. One transmitter of 150 KW.
6. 15 transmitters of 100 KW each.
7. Two transmitters of 50 KW each.
8. 211 transmitters of 20 KW each.
9. One transmitter of 10 KW.

This, it is hoped, will enable the stations, to give more time, at popular listening hours to their own programmes more suited to the linguistic and cultural needs of the area."[32]

"AIR had proposed an expenditure of 559 crores for its 10 year perspective plan out of which Rs. 275 crores were to be utilised during the Sixth Plan. However, the Planning Commission agreed only for 122.38 crores. This resulted in postponement of new stations in the number of states.

The projects already completed and installed during the first four years of the Sixth Plan, i.e., 1-4-1980 to 31-3-1984 include:

1. Introduction of FM (Frequency Modulation) at Calcutta and Bombay.

2. Commissioning of a 10 KW SW transmitter at Aizwal on August 15th, 1982 and 100 KW MW transmitters at Delhi and Cuddapah.

3. Permanent studios were brought into regular use at Jeypore, Agartala, Najibadbad, Allahabad, Siliguri, Coimbatore, Gwalior, Dharwar, Jodhpur and Ranchi.

4. Opening of a new station at Gangtok with 10 KWMW transmitter on 2-10-1982. (AIR's 86th Centre.)"[33]

Due to the cuts in proposals, the scheme of Local Radio was considerably reduced. However, 6 centres were proposed in the Sixth Plan and a beginning was made with the foundation stone laying at Adilabad and Kota.

By the end of the Sixth Plan, about 95% of the population and 86% of the area in the country was covered by the medium wave service.[34]

Seventh Plan

The project to instal 'Local Radio' is still under implementation. It had been decided to instal more than 100 transmitters in different districts on priority basis, during the period of Seventh Plan. Construction of Studio Buildings started at places where foundation stone laying was done during the Sixth Plan period. The places include Adilabad, Diphu, Koinjhar, Kota, Guna, Khandwa, Sholapur, Betul etc. However, the allocation made by the International Telecommunication Union to instal 352 low power transmitters will only be completed by the end of Eighth Plan, if adequate funds are provided.

Projects to raise the powers of few regional stations is also under implementation and few stations will be provided with FM transmitters to reduce the interference during the night service.

National Channel

The infrastructure for the National Channel has been built-up which includes the provision of a Mega Watt transmitter at Nagpur. This project has been completed. This is a great landmark in the history of broadcasting in our country. The National Service from Nagpur was inaugurated on 19th May, 1988, with its studios at Delhi in the Jawaharlal Nehru Stadium. Earlier National and other important programmes were broadcast on one of the main channels of Delhi Station and were relayed by other stations to increase the coverage of important programmes. With the result regional and zonal stations were not having sufficient time to their own programmes of regional and zonal importance. This National Service 'will be followed by a chain of other transmitters to relay these programmes, thus providing a powerful National Channel reaching most parts of the country.'[35]

News Services Division

The News Services of All India Radio came into existence in 1937 as the Central News Organisation. Prior to this, news bulletins were broadcast from few stations but the work was not organised on a professional basis.

At present, it is putting-out 68 bulletins of a duration of 10 hours 8 minutes daily in 10 Indian languages in its home service.[36]

External Services Division

All India Radio, started its External Broadcasting soon after the outbreak of the Second World War, on 1st October, 1939, when it started a service in Pashtu for the listeners across the north-west frontier.

In 1970, External Services put out programmes in 21 languages with a total duration of 46 hours 12 minutes in a day. In 1982, the number of languages rose to 25 (17 foreign languages including English and 8 Indian languages) and total hours of transmission rose to 56 hours 45 minutes.

To project India's rich and glorious culture, Indian Music is broadcast in ample measures and about one-third of the total duration, is devoted to Indian Music.[37]

Total Hours Broadcast and Percentage of Music Programmes

Rapid growth in the radiation power of the transmiters and opening of new stations, has resulted in increase in broadcasting hours with a variety of programmes.

The statistics of 1937-38 show that about 74% of the total broadcast hours was devoted to music while the present figure is about 40%. This shows that when total transmission of music items increased many fold, the percentage on the other hand reduced.[38]

"During 1960, AIR's total programme output was 1,08,256 hours and 14 mts. (Excluding Vividh Bharati programmes which occupied 7,123 hours mostly music). Music output was for 50,981 hours 28 mts. i.e. 46.06% of the total broadcast time in general programmes. In 1961, AIR's total broadcast time was 1,17,265 hours of which, 7,931 hours was takenup by Vividh Bharati leaving a balance of 1,09,334 hours. Total music time during 1961 (including 2,107 hours of Western Music) came to 51,184 hours which works out to 46.7 of the total. The programmes of special audiences like children, women, rural dwellers, armed forces etc. amounted to 21.47% of the total programmes comprising various items approximately half of which are music. Thus, the total music output of AIR's programmes of 1961 would be any where between 55 to 60%."[39]

Out of the total music programmes of AIR, the ratio of various music items in 1961 was:-

1. Classical Music—Vocal and Instrumental 52%
2. Folk Music 3%
3. Light Music 26%
4. Devotional Music 12%
5. Film Music 7%

(Excluding 2000 hours of Western Music which amounts to 4%).[40]

The total duration of Vividh Bharati programmes was 7,931 hours out of which 90% was devoted to music (70% film music and 20% light devotional, folk and classical music).

Increase in Total Hours but Decrease in Percentage (Music Programmes)

"In the course of time, total transmission hours of the home service and Vividh Bharati increased many fold. Statistics of the year 1975 shows that total broadcast hours of AIR programmes were 4,38,680 hours, out of which 1,41,198 hours were taken by Vividh Bharati, i.e. 400 percent increase in the transmission hours. Considering 2,97,481 hours of home service, the percentage of classical music (Vocal and Instrumental) was 15.8, folk music, 3.2, light music 9.9, devotional music 4.7, film music 5.4 and Western music 1.8."[41] And the total duration of music programmes was 1,21,285 hours, which constitutes about 40.8% of the total programmes of the home service. Hence percentage of classical music calculated in music programmes was about 39.

Analysis of these figures and comparison with 1961 figures show that the total duration of the music programmes increased four folds, but percentage of classical music was reduced, both in comparison with total broadcast hours as well as in total music programmes. This study shows that in the course of 14 years, percentage of classical music came down from 46.7 to 40.7 in total broadcast hours and from 52 to 39 percent in music programmes respectively. (Appendix-Tables 3 to 7).

The reasons for this reduction in percentage of classical music programmes are well known. First, "Except for a few years when listeners, in north particularly felt that too much of classical music was being given, or rather imposed on them, different types of music, light, folk, devotional and classical have settled down today to reasonable relative proportions,"[42] wrote Shri Luthra, and the second is the introduction of new spoken-word and special audience programmes replacing music programmes. The number of news bulletins have also been increased considerably. The only alternative to introduce such programmes, without increasing total transmission hours, was the curtailment of music programmes, that too, classical music, for which liking and listening is low. Music programmes gets a kick always with the introduction of any new spokenword item as there is no corresponding increase in transmission hours, thus reduction in percentage.

This trend is continuing. The figures of 1982, as compared with those of 1980 show that the percentage of music programmes, as compared to the total transmission hours, was further reduced from 40.7 to 36.11 and percentage of classical music programmes, as compared with total music programmes, was downed from 39 to 33.46% [43], while total transmission hours of music programmes increased.

Another factor, which is responsible for decreasing percentage of the music items is that most of AIR stations are single channel stations and all types of programmes like play, features, News, talks and music, special relays from Delhi or regional stations are to be accommodated on the same channel, hence any new programme introduced or relayed, leads to reduction in music hours.

However, quantitative increase does not always popularise any programme. The pattern of broadcasting classical music is continuing as per policy directives of earlier period. National programmes, Tuesday night concerts, Radio Sangeet Sammelan and other regular programmes of regional and local stations are doing well and there are regular listeners to such programmes. In addition, regional stations have also started special programmes like regional concerts. With the growth of Radio stations, the total hours of broadcast of classical music have been crossed doubled in thirty-two years:

Year	*No. of Radio Stations*	*Total hours of Classical Music*
1961	30	27000
1975	71	47097
1982	86	52143
1993	148	60000 Approx

That means, people of whole India are exposed to more than 59000 hours of listening, which no institution of any kind can provide. So far the quality of these programmes is concerned, AIR is still maintaining its standards by inviting graded artists. Not only quality of the performance has improved, technical quality has also been standardised with the use of modern equipments.

Research and Development

In broadcasting, technical quality of the performance plays an important role in attention holding of the listener. Whatever is being performed in the studios, should reach the listener audiable and clear. The journey of the programme from the mike to the radio set, passes through the number of technical equipments like, mixer, amplifier, transmission lines and transmitter etc.

The technical problems in many ways faced from the beginning of the broadcasting. "Before broadcasting began, virtually the only microphones were those used in telephones, designed to transmit a limited range of frequencies, and to be held close to the mouth. The earliest broadcasts were, in fact, made with the aid of such microphones, sometimes with a small horn added to increase sensitivity."[44] With the result, the quality of the performance was not as good as it is today. Continuous efforts of the researchers made it possible that the crystal clear programmes broadcast or relayed, finally received at the listener's end.

The Research and Development wing of AIR deals with the technical problems. "The activities of the department are broadly of three types: (i) Studios and investigations of various problems relating to sound and television, (ii) Research and Development of equipment including proto-type production, and (iii) Rendering operational and technical services to the network."[45]

Acoustics and audio are the most important factors in the sound broadcasting, particularly in the case of music programmes. "The activities of the Engineering Research Department are carried out in four sections devoted to propagation, acoustics and audio-engineering, proto-type production and design and development. Some notable work has been done on noise and longwave propagation, rainfall extenuating margins in the 12 GH band for satellite broadcasting system, the dynamic range of Indian Music and musical instruments and solid state FM link transmitters."[46]

Moreover, 'AIR and Doordarshan have a Technical Advisory Committee presided over by a distinguished scientist which includes persons from National Laboratories and other scientific bodies who are experts in their fields. The function of this committee is to advise AIR/Doordarshan on research and development programmes with reference to work in progress in other research institutions.'[47]

The most important and latest development in the history of Indian broadcasting is the use of RN Channel of Insat-IB, and ID, for the purpose of relaying news and National programmes and other important national events. With this advancement *the quality of music programmes has improved during the relay from Delhi by other stations.* Prior to this, National and other programmes were relayed through air links, hence the quality of the programmes was not satisfactory and sometimes it was unbearable. "Two RN uplinks at Delhi have been operationalised and simplified, Revive Terminals have been installed at 28 centres. This has brought about an improvement in the quality of relay programmes and news from Delhi."[48]

With the development of new equipments by the Research and Development, today, the journey of the programme from the microphone to the receiver set at the listener's end, has become more convenient.

Audience Research and Listeners' Profile

In a developing country like India, the responsibility of a broadcasting organisation is more complex than those in the developed countries. It has to maintain the standard of the programmes, and also has to fulfil the requirements of a layman. For this purpose, a great care has to be taken while planning and producing programmes. "While it should avoid playing to the gallery, at the same time, it has also to see that as far as possible, it should project good taste because good taste and public taste are sometimes not concurrent. In less developed countries like India, the divergence between the two is more sharp that in the case of countries where the gulf which separates the layman from the expert is insignificant. Naturally, therefore, the task of planning attractive broadcast programmes for an audience whose taste vary a great deal, becomes all the more difficult."[49] In such cases, planning of broadcasts can only be done on an experimental basis and feedback from the audience can only prove the success of a broadcaster. Listeners' response, sometimes, compelled the authorities to make necessary changes in the programme policy. The birth of Vividh Bharati service is an ideal example in this regard. It is important for a broadcasting organisation like AIR to find out whether programmes broadcast for a particular type of audience are gaining ground or losing it.

"Again the BBC has clearly recognised that while Audience Research Data should be available to programme planners and the general public, programme policy should not be dictated by the 'Box Office'."[50]

Listeners' research in India is more complex due to different cultural zones: "India has a number of cultural zones with marked characteristics. Fourteen major languages and about 200 dialects are spoken throughout the length and breadth of the country. Customs, habits, religious practices, local fairs and festivals lend a colourful diversity to the social milieu prevailing in the country. Therefore, it is necessary for a planner of radio programmes to have a good understanding of the social, cultural, religious and educational interests of listeners residing in the various zones. Added to this are the problems pertaining to the people residing in rural areas scattered in 6 lakh villages."[51]

In order to know listeners' reaction a survey, first time, was conducted by Delhi station in 1936 by issuing a questionaire to 1500 licence holders asking them whether they found the programme timing satisfactory, were interested in classical or light music (and if so, in which forms especially Khayal, Thumri, Ghazal, Dadra or Qawali) who their favourite artists were, which artist they dislike, and if they would like more talks, music, drama and news...." 650 replies were received, which was thought to be very encouraging. An analysis of these showed that about *one-third of the listeners appreciated classical music*, while the rest expressed a strong dislike of it, there was almost unanimous approval of the timings of the broadcast, 'ghazal' was by far the most popular, with 'Qawwali' the next in order and 'Khayal' at the bottom of the preference list. It was seen that more than 50% of the Indian listeners listened to and appreciated European music and there was a general desire for more and better drama."[52]

A similar survey was conducted by Bombay station "in May, 1938 and a system of maintaining detailed statistics of appreciation and 'criticism' contained in listeners' letters, reactions appearing in press and interviews with the representatives of the public, was started in October, 1938. "[53] All this was maintained by the Station Directors and a weekly analysis was sent to the Headquarters. There was no such unit or wing independently looking after the work of analysing listeners reactions and maintaining periodical record.

The organised listeners' research started only after World War II,..."it was felt by the authorities that for proper planning of programmes, listener research should be organised on regular lines and a beginning was made in 1946. Six out of the nine stations then in existence were provided with Listener Research Unit, each under the charge of a Listener Research Officer....The work at the stations was coordinated by a Central cell in the Directorate General (headed by an Assistant Director, Listener Research first appointed in September 1948, which issued necessary instructions and guided research."[54]

At present there is a Director of Audience Research who "draws up the schedule of surveys for the year, on the basis of proposals received from Units....Studies of a somewhat similar nature are taken up at several places in the country at about the same time to ensure uniformity of approach, objectives, methodology, reference period and thereby the comparability of data."[55]

Surveys conducted on the basis of 'random samples' which now became difficult due to the decision of the Govt. in 1981 to de-licence two band sets and later all sets, because the post office would no longer have the names and addresses of owners of such sets. But the surveys conducted surely prove, that the popularity of the classical music programmes have increased. The drive, which was started in 1952-53 to popularise this art form, was really successful.

Listening of Music Programmes (Analysis)

It is very difficult to assess the accurate and exact figures about the listening of any programme and its popularity. But the increasing number of radio sets, and percentage listening (based on sample surveys) are two important indicators of popularity of any programme. It is a fact, that this institution in India could reach about 95% (now 100%) of population, especially in remote areas where it is rather impossible for any other media. In every section of society, variety of listeners are present, and variety of programmes have their own listening choices. It is also an undisputed fact that the maximum number of listeners are music lovers, and a small fraction of such listeners is inclined to classical music.

With the increase in the number of transmitters and radio sets, the number of listeners increased, even if the percentage listening remain same. For example, if the listening *of classical music programmes remain constant at 19% in the course of years, there were 190 listeners when the radio sets were only 1000. When the number of radio sets rose to 1,00,00,000 (one crore), naturally with 19% listening, total number of listeners will be 19,00,000 (nineteen lakhs).* This is what happened with the listening of classical music programmes.

The listeners of classical music can be divided into the following categories:-

(a) Listeners, know nothing about classical music, but enjoy listening indirectly because they like it (even if they do not know why) due to the impact of light and film music.

(b) Listeners, who know little about classical music and enjoy light classical and 'Chhota Khayal' etc.

(c) Students of classical music.

(d) Musicians, artists, musicologists and their disciples.

Listening of Vividh Bharati (Classical Music)

Vividh Bharati programmes in India have record listening. A survey conducted in 1980, reveals that in urban areas, it is 69% on week days and 77% on Sundays. The programmes are equally popular in rural areas and listening is 73% on week days and 67% on Sundays. Coming to the listening of classical music programmes of Vividh Bharati, Sangeet Sarita can be said to be best listened programme. Its listening is 18 to 20% in urban areas and 8 to 13% in rural areas. These figures are taken from field survey of Delhi, which is also approximately equal to All India figures.

While more than 95% population is covered by our transmitters, it can be easily calculated what 18 or 20% means. This will be equal to several millions listeners of different age group and social status. This programme Sangeet Sarita is not only popular in north India, but also equally popular in all the corners of the country with a varying degree. This could be possible through film music.

The popularity of film or light music does not, necessarily means, that the listening of classical music is not considerably increasing. Even if, this figure of 19% is maintained, we still have millions of listeners increasing with the growth of radio sets and radio stations in India. Even in European and other countries, listening of classical music has increased due to radio. "Despite the attraction of jazz from the commercial service, the Australian Broadcasting Commission have found that audiences for classical music programmes have always been on increase," wrote Mr. Awasthy, "Our own experience with the commercial service of Radio Ceylon has also been similar. Initially, no doubt, this service took away a number of listeners from AIR. But it is interesting to note that Ceylon has recently been putting out performances by some of the top artists of Indian Classical Music. Moreover, in Ceylon itself, there has been considerable criticism of the commercial setup. It was contended that, whereas AIR has done a great deal for the furtherance of Indian culture and provided opportunities for Indian artists, Radio Ceylon had merely been patronising cheap foreign music."[56]

Growth in listening of any programme can be assessed by (i) Number of Radio sets (ii) Listeners survey to come out with the figures of percentage listening and (iii) Listeners' letters. A detailed study of all the three factors is necessary to assess the increased popularity of Indian classical music.

(i) Number of Radio Sets

"When Lord Irwin inaugurated the Bombay station on 23rd July, 1927 (followed by Calcutta on 26th August 1927), the total number of licenced listeners in India was estimated to be less than 1000. The end of the year saw these rise 3,594."[57] By the end of 1938, the number of radio licences increased to 64,480. (For yearly figures see Appendix table 10). At the time of Independence, there were 2,75,955 radio licences in India which comes to less than 2% of what it is to-day. The growth rate increased considerably since 1950 to 1960 and at the end of 1960, the total number of radio licences reached to 21,42,754, i.e. nine times more than that of 1947. Even than, the percentage as compared from the 1985 figures (approximately 3,20,00,000) remains some 7.

The growth rate increased markedly from 1960 to 1970 and the figures reached to 1,18,36,653. During this period two landmarks were established. (i) The appreciable growth of number of transmitters, followed by the increase in the population and area covered (area 28 to 68% and population 55 to 80%) and (ii) availability of transistors, i.e. cheap radio sets suiting the pockets of the lower middle and lower class. During this period more medium wave transmitters were installed to fulfil the demand of lowcost sets owners. This was the period when cultural revolution really started in the country and the broadcasting which was limited to elite class till Independence, later spread to middle and lower class, and now reached to masses and the broadcasters were forced to revise their policies. Rescheduling of Vividh Bharati programmes was also carried out during this period.

Since then, the growth continued till the end of 1983, when expansion of television transmitters started. The maximum number of radio licences was assessed in 1979, when it was 2,06,74,113.[58] Later in 1981, Govt. took a decision to delicence two band sets and later in 1984 all the sets were freed from licence fee. Hence it is very difficult to assess exact number of radio sets. But taking in view the last progress and popularity of lowcost sets, according to P.C. Chatterjee, the total number of radio sets in the country is around 60 millions (in 1988).[59] Taking in view the 1981-82 figures of 19% listening of classical music, the total number of listeners would run into millions.

(ii) Listeners' survey reports

If the reports of the Listeners surveys conducted during the course of years are analysed, it is evident that the listening of the classical music is beyond satisfaction. The all India figures in 1936 were about 30%. Over the years, the percentage of classical music has declined from 18.4% in 1965 to 12.12% in 1980. However, the total number of listeners, and hours broadcast increased many fold due to fast expansion of broadcasting facilities. "Listening of classical music on an all India basis worked out to 19.8% in Urban areas and 7.8% in rural area."[60] Taking in view the socio-economic structure, the listening percentage is more than satisfactory.

There is another factor which may also be taken into consideration. The listening at home on radio is regular, while going to the concert halls is occasional. It will be appropriate to mention here that BBC continues its programme even if the listening is 2% or less, because 2% in 100 millions means 2 million people. Hence even 10% listening on an average on all India basis means, out of 100 million listeners, 19 millions are regularly tuned to classical music programmes broadcast from AIR. These figures do not include listening of our programmes in other countries.

Impact of Literacy

The figures shown in table 16 also reveal some other important factors. The listening of light and film music is maximum (around 80%) in all zones. However, the listening of classical music is less in north and central zones (around 8 to 10% in urban and 3.6 to 3.9% in rural areas), while in East, West and South zones, listening of classical music is more. (21.5, 17.2 and 34.9% in urban and 9.3, 7.4. and 12.7% in rural areas respectively.) This shows that the percentage listening of classical music is directly related with the literacy figures and socio-economic status.[61]

(iii) Listeners' letters

It is a question open to debate, whether listeners response, through their letters can be treated as an indication of the popularity and success of any programme. However, one thing is sure that whatever reaction is shown by the audience, at least the programme is being listened. How can a person write without listening ? One more thing which is important in this context is that not even 2% of the listeners write letters. If centpercent listeners will start writing, the buildings of AIR will be flooded with the letters and disposal will be another problem. Another fact which is revealed by the close examination of these letters is "that the vast majority are nothing but requests for favourite songs, and queries sent with the obvious purpose of hearing their names read over microphone, in reply of letters and other such features. The proportion of letters commenting on the quality of programmes or making suggestions based on intelligent listening or viewing is almost negligible."[62]

Asa Briggs, the writer of the Birth of Broadcasting, thinks in a different manner "what are listeners' letters really worth? Letters are written for the most part by ego-maniacs, cranks, axe-grinders or the incorrigibly idles who can find nothing better to do. Analysis of letters is not the same thing as analysis of listeners' (real or supposed) preference......the main object should be to find out who the listeners is, and when he listened to this and that sort of material- in other words to establish an electoral register not to carry out a plebiscite."[63]

However, increasing number of listeners' letters indicates popularly of the programme. The tradition of assessing listeners' taste by inviting their views, was started with the beginning of broadcasting. The number of listeners letters increased many folds since Independence and in 1980, 20,34,500 letters were received by the Home Service of AIR. In 1983, the figure rose to 29,54,910. The figures are really appreciable.

The highest percentage of these letters goes to the request programmes and film music programmes, as the listeners are interested in their names on radio. Taking in view this tendency of the listeners a number of stations started request programmes for other categories of music items.

Even Vividh Bharti Service, in order to popularise classical music programmes started a weekly request programme of classical music under the title 'Anuranjini' for half an hour from 3:15 p.m. to 3:45 p.m., although, the number of letters received is less than those received for film music, the listening of this programme has increased due to this experiment.

This Assessment clearly shows, that the number of listeners of classical and light classical music programmes has since increased. It is almost impossible to come out with acurate number of listeners but the fact remains that number of listeners run into millions.

References

1. G.C. Awasthy, *Broadcasting in India*, p. 11.
2. K.S. Duggal, *Indian Broadcasting Media*, p. 3.
3. G.C. Awasthy, *Broadcasting in India*, p. 11.
4. *Ibid.*, p. 12.
5. H.R. Luthra, *Indian Broadcasting*, p. 199.
6. Edited from G. C. Awasthy's, *Broadcasting in India*, p. 12.
7. H.R.Luthra, Indian Broadcasting, p. 200.
8. G.C. Awasthy, *Broadcasting in India*, p. 12.
9. *Ibid.*
10. *Ibid.*, p. 16.
11. H.R. Luthra, *Indian Broadcasting*, p. 202.
12. G.C. Awasthi, *Broadcasting in India*.
13. K.S. Duggal, *Indian Broadcasting Media*, p. 3.
14. *Ibid* p. 19.
15. *Ibid.*, p. 19.
16. *Ibid.*
17. *Ibid.*, pp. 19-20.
18. G. C. Awasthy, *Broadcasting in India*, p. 27.
19. *H.R. Luthra, Indian Broadcosting*, p. 202.

20. *Ibid.*, pp. 205 and 207.
21. *Ibid.*
22. *Ibid.*, pp. 206 and 207.
23. *Ibid.*, p. 213.
24. K.S. Duggal, *Indian Broadcast Media*, p. 6.
25. H.R. Luthra, *Indian Broadcasting*, p. 213.
26. K.S. Duggal, *Indian Broadcast Media*, p. 6.
27. H.R. Luthra, *Indian Broadcasting*, p. 215.
28. *Ibid.*
29. K.S. Duggal, *Indian Broadcast Media*, p. 6.
30. H.R. Luthra, *Indian Broadcasting*, p. 218.
31. *Ibid.*, p. 219.
32. *Ibid.*, p. 220.
33. *Ibid.*, p. 222.
34. K.S. Duggal, *Indian Broadcast Media*, pp. 6-7.
35. *Mass Media in India*, 1984 published by the Publication Division of Ministry of I&B.
36. K.S. Duggal, *Indian Broadcast Media*, p. 7.
37. *Ibid.*, pp. 8-9.
38. H.R. Luthra, *Indian Broadcasting*, p. 298.
39. G.C. Awasthy, *Broadcasting in India*, p. 33.
40. G.C. Awasthy, *Broadcasting in India*, From chapter 'Music Items'.
41. *Mass Media in India*, 1978, Publication Division, Ministry of I&B.
42. H.R. Luthra, *Indian Broadcasting*, p. 299.
43. *Mass Media in India*, 1981-83, Publication Division, Ministry of I&B, p. 137.
44. Keith Geddes, *Broadcasting in Britain*, p. 14.
45. *Mass Media in India*, 1984, Publication Division, Ministry of I&B., p. 30.
46. P.C. Chatterjee, *Broadcasting in India*, p. 84.
47. *Ibid.*, p. 85.
48. *Mass Media in India*, 1984, Publication Division, Ministry of I&B, p. 30.
49. G.C. Awasthy, *Broadcasting in India*, p. 202.
50. *Ibid.*, p. 220.
51. *Ibid.*, p. 216.
52. H.R. Luthra, *Indian Broadcasting*, pp. 461-62.
53. *Ibid.*
54. *Ibid.*, pp. 463-66.
55. *Ibid.*
56. G.C. Awasthy, *Broadcasting in India*, p. 219.
57. *Ibid.*, p. 258.

58. Figures from (i) G.C. Awasthy's *Broadcasting in India* and K.S. Duggal's *Indian Broadcast Media,* and *Mass Media in India,* 1983-84.
59. P.C. Chatterjee's Article in *Daily Hindustan Times* dated 3-3-1988.
60. U.L. Baruah, *This is All India Radio*, p. 48.
61. Calculated from Table-16 (Appendix).
62. H.R. Luthra, *Indian Broadcasting*, p. 469.
63. *Ibid.*

8

Analysis of Facilities to the Artists: Merits and Demerits

Artist

Artist—music or otherwise—is the pivot of all programming, broadcast or staged. No amount of administration or well designed studios can make a good broadcasting without artist. Technical facilities and good management may improve the performance provided the basic artist is good. To maintain the quality and high standards a number of factors are to be taken care of.

A variety of artists are working for AIR. There are announcers, comperes, news readers, script writers, drama voicers, talkers, producers and musicians etc. So far as the production of music programmes is concerned, the artists working are composers, musicians, instrumentalists and music producers. AIR artists can be divided into two categories: (i) Staff Artists, who are working on a regular basis drawing monthly salary appointed on a contract, and (ii) Casual Artists, who are invited for a particular performance and paid a consolidated fee for each programme.

Staff Artist

Before Independence, there was no such policy to recruit artists on regular basis in AIR. It was a matter of direct negotiation between an artist and the station director for a contract on assignment basis. There was no such audition board or system for gradation. Even after Independence, artists were appointed on monthly contract on a consolidated fee and these contracts were renewed after proper assessment of their performance.

"After the war, in 1946-47, the fee of staff artists ranged from about 80 to 1000 per month depending on the merit.... If the station director felt the need of, say an additional tabla player, or announcer, he appointed a person on a contract which was renewable from month to month. The selection was made from among the persons on the station's list who had some experience of broadcasting. After this trial period of monthly contract, the station was expected to obtain the sanction of the Director General for the artist's appointment as a staff artist. Inspite of these instructions a number of persons were engaged for years on monthly contracts. One of the very good things accomplished by the late P.M. Lad during his short tenure as Secretary to the Ministry of I&B, was to put an end to this nefarious practice."[1]

Since 1960, rules for appointment of Staff Artists were framed. All vacancies were advertised in press or over radio and selection committees were formed. For higher posts like Asstt. Producer, Producer, Deputy Chief Producers and Chief Producers, there was a provision for one non-official member, on selection committees.

Earlier service benefits, during the period of contract, were not clearly specified. In 1956, other benefits like leave, medical benefits, gratuity, maternity leave to women artists were provided like other regular government servants. However, fee continued to be fixed.

Still there was uncertainty in the service career. The period of contract was only for a period of one to three years and its renewal was wholly on the discretion of the Station Director. Their contract was terminable at any time. Monthly fee in those days used to be Rs.150/- to 300/- per month according to the grades, without any increment during the period of contract. "Prior to 1955, some 'C' class musicians were employed (if those with better gradings were not available) and such persons were given monthly salaries between Rs.120/- to 150/- per month. Under the present rules no musician graded less than 'B' is normally to be employed and yet fee offered is only Rs.150/- ."[2]

Unemployment and poor economic condition forced them to work in AIR, as there was no other choice. 'Ten or fifteen years of specialised service in AIR renders them unfit for any alternative employment. With nothing to look forward to, it is not surprising that they should become indifferent to their work.'[3] wrote Mr. Awasthy in 1962.....'Thus a sort of cold war has developed between the administration and staff artists, and I believe that this is an important factor in the deterioration of quality of work which we have been witnessing in the last few years....'

In early sixties, conditions changed little when the artists were given specified pay scales and period of contract was also extended to 5 years. "With effect from the 1st October, 1964, they were given a new deal of being granted all the allowances admissible to government servants."[4]

Further in 1971, revised fee scales were introduced on the basis of the recommendation made by the departmental study team and by the SIU (Staff Inspection Unit) of the Finance Ministry. "Staff artists were also made eligible for overtime and interim relief (to offset the increased cost of living), like other government employees. In 1973-74, it was decided that subject to a review at the age of 58 years, all staff artists of AIR on the 'sound' side would be retained in service upto the age of 60 years. In June, 1976, further revision of salary scales took place on the analogy of the recommendations of the Third Pay Commission for regular government employees."[5] By this time all the staff artists were given contracts upto the age of 58 years with new fee scales and other facilities like yearly increment, medical attendence, bonus, residential accommodation, children education allowance and other benefits available to the regular government servants from time to time.

Till 1983, all the categories were treated as staff artists whether performing or engaged in production. "On the basis of the recommendations of the Media Advisory Committee headed by Shri G. Parthasarthy, the Government have decided to categorise Staff Artists into two classes, one which (those engaged on production of programmes) would be entitled to pension, and other (those who actually face microphone) to Contributory Provident Fund. In this context, steps were initiated to equate the Producers and other in the staff artists production cadre at appropriate levels with regular staff."[6] Producers are equated with Programme Executives and Production assistants, editors and script writers with the cadre of Transmission Executives.

According to new policy, the performing artists will be recruited for 5 years contract now and the renewal of their contract will depend on the further screening. Artists, who are working at present on 58 years contract are asked to opt for five years contract, where they will get pension also. "A liberalisation of pension entitlement of staff artists was announced by the Ministry of I&B on August, 30,1983 to take effect from September, 1,1983."[7] But only few of the artists already working on 58 years contract have opted under the new scheme, as their service is less secured.

At present, staff artists are availing better facilities and drawing respectable salaries according to their grades as compared to 1961 conditions. They are availing almost all the benefits provided to the regular government servants, and their strength have increased considerably. In 1961, the total strength of staff artists was on 1400, which was 3000 in 1983. However, this increase is not with the parity of the increasing number of radio stations:

Year	*No. of Radio Stns.*	*No. of S.A.s*
1961	30	1400
1983	90	3000[8]

Casual Artists

In addition to more than 3000 staff artists, on the roll, there are approximately more than 27000 approved casual artists booked regularly by All India Radio from time to time on assignment basis. While much has been done to improve the conditions of the regular staff artists, the conditions in the case of casual artists remain unchanged since long. However, due to the status and popularity, provided by AIR, number of casual artists of different grades have increased since Independence.

The role of programme staff in AIR is not only to plan and produce programmes, but also to scout new talent outside AIR and prepare a panel of such artists. "For this they must not only get the best out of each talker, writer, singer or other performer, but also be continually looking for fresh talent."[9]

Even in thirties and forties the stations were asked "to maintain individual card index of all types of performers giving their personal data such as special interest, voice quality, accent, fees and dates of 'bookings'. In the case of music artists, relevant information would also include the type of music, extent of repertoire and Gharana etc. if any."[10] Later after 1952, new audition system came into force to screen the artists of different grades.

With the growing interest of listeners, the number of artists also increased to provide variety in classical music programmes "yet AIR has remained committed to providing for not only the growing number of classical music artists on its roll but also for a fare based on music available on tapes and discs."[11]

Let us analyse the role of AIR in increasing the number of performing artists during the course of years. There were 36 staff artists employed in AIR in 1939 at Delhi station. The figures of other stations are not tracable, as there were only six radio stations, but the total number was not more than 100 in any case. At present there are more than 3000 regular staff artists and some 2753 casual artists of Hindustani Music of different grades on the approved list of AIR, (as on 1-1-82) out of the total of 27786, of different variety of music.[12]

Type of music	*Top*	*A*	*B-High*	*B*	*Total*
Hindustani	66	404	1044	1239	2753
Karnatak	51	492	1119	1362	3024
Light	17	355	1358	7168	8838
Folk	1	32	350	1239	12744
Western	–	11	51	365	427

During 1979-81, over three thousand music artists were added in 25 major stations.

Analysis of fee paid

To attract the outside talent for the purpose of programmes, fee paid plays an important role in maintaining the quality and standards. AIR has played a discriminating role in the case of casual artists from its beginning. "Imagine, a musician of the greatness of Ustad Allauddin Khan or Ustad Mushtaq Hussain Khan being made to broadcast three or four times a day for a total fee of 70 or 80 rupees", wrote Narayan Menon..."It was an insult to the musician and to his profession."[13] This was the condition in pre-Independence days, what one can imagine for ordinary and local artists. In those days- "a few musicians received fees in excess of Rs.150....Many others of note were paid something in the neighbourhood of Rs.100."[14] Even now, the situation has not much changed. The views of Mr. Luthra are also similar in this regard: "Fees paid to broadcasters are an important factor in maintaining a good standard of programme out put. In this respect, mainly because of financial constraints, AIR has not, from the beginning, been a liberal paymaster."[15]

In 1953, fees of the music artists were fixed according to their grades, which was revised in 1970. Even than, the fee of B grade artist remain below hundred, those B-High and A grade were getting Rs.150 to 250 for each performance of about one hour. Fees were again revised in 1981 by 50 to 70% due to the income from Commercial Broadcasting, which was deposited into 'Non- Lapsable Fund'.

Fee Table of Music Artists[16]

Year	*Top*	*A*	*B-High*	*B*
1981	500	250- 400	125-200	75-120
1985	750	350- 500	200-275	100-160
1989	1500	600-1000	350-500	50-300
T.A. and D.A. Extra				

In February 1989, fee of different grades have further revised with a increase from 50 to 75%, still Mr. Baruah, Ex-DG, AIR was not satisfied, "In music too artists like Ravi Shanker, Ali Akbar Khan, M.S. Subbalaxmi and others in that class command for their public appearances fee ten times or more than what AIR or TV can give them even now."[17] With the result, such artists sometimes refuse to accept the broadcast offered by AIR. In some cases, programme officers and producers are able to manage their recordings on their personal efforts.

In the beginning, when broadcasting was a new experiment artists were attracted to AIR not because of the payment, but for the purpose of their publicity and fame. "It is true, that the wide publicity which mass media can bring does count with performances but the enability of Akashvani and Doordarshan to offer special fee for really outstanding talent, be it musicians or talkers (and not just the maximum of the normal prescribed scales) has resulted in the general reluctance of such people to accept engagements, except occasionally when approached personally and especially persuaded to do so."[18]

The situation in the case of less popular artists and new talent is little different. They accept such offers immediately without caring for the fee paid. There are many such examples where artists are accepting such offers without fail even if they are away from the station and they come to attend their scheduled broadcast on their own. Some artists of high repute, who started their career from the studios of AIR still respect AIR's offer.

In any case, casual artists of AIR are not getting sufficient share from the total allocations, which is evident from the facts and figures given below:

"Out of its total annual grant of 1938, AIR spent approximately 31% on programmes; by 1968, the percentage had dropped to 17. But even from this reduced allocation, the greater part is spent on salaries of staff artists. The figures given below show how much some stations of AIR spent in 1968-69 on fees for musicians, talkers, writers and others not on their staff:"[19]

Station	*Total prog. expenditure in lakhs*	*Amount spent on staff artists*	*Amount spent on outside artists*
Calcutta	9.5	6.3	3.2
Madras	8.0	6.5	1.5
Delhi	15.8	11.9	3.9
Vijaywada	2.7	2.5	0.2
Srinagar	4.4	4.2	0.2

The following tables show the ratio of expenditure on programmes, as compared with the total expenditure, which has fallen over the years:[20]

Year	*Expenditure on Programmes (a)*	*Total expenditure on service (b)*	*Ratio of (a) to (b)*
1936-37	3,34,964	9,28,023	36%
1937-38	4,17,125	13,00,029	31%
1938-39	6,36,142	20,55,252	31%
1965-66	1,30,46,000	6,74,48,000	19%
1971-72	2,35,53,000	16,41,97,000	14%

Since the figures under (b) also includes the salaries paid to regular staff artists, it does not show how much of it was paid to talent booked from outside. Recently, figures are being presented in a way which makes this clear, while the account sheets continue in other aspects to appear as baffling as before to laymen. In 1977-78 fee paid to staff artists was 7.85% of the total expenditure while those paid to casual artists described as 'payment for professionals and specialists service was 3.61% adding to a total of 11.46%. This, apart from being too low, and perhaps lowest ever, also shows that persons employed by AIR itself had twice as much money spent on them as was disbursed to outside talent. Corresponding figures of later years are:'[21]

Year	*Fee for staff artists*	*Outside talent*	*Total*
1979-80	9.0%	5.1%	14.1%
1980-81	8.6%	4.7%	13.3%
1981-82	9.1%	5.4%	14.5%
1982-83	8.7%	6.5%	15.2%

This works to an average of 14.2% which seems quite low for any broadcasting organisation, but the consolation is that it has not gone down since 1971 and the steep decline of the earlier years (during which it fell from 31% in 1937-38 to 14% within 25 years) has been arrested.

The above figures clearly show that the casual artists are hardly getting their share from the organisation. This may also be observed in day to day working in AIR. A, B-high grade artist employed as staff artist gets around Rs. 2000 to 3000 per month, while a casual artist of the same grade is booked once in a month for a fee of Rs. 350/- or so. This factor becomes more important in the case of music artists as AIR is only cultural organisation where less popular and local artists can find a platform for their future progress.

In this context, it is not important how much money is spent, but how it is spent is more important. If the ratio of total expenditure is properly shared on programmes, there can be a good quality production even with the same money. Imagine 3000 staff artists are paid some 9%, while 27,700 casual artists are getting only 5% if the total 14% spent on programmes.

At present, transfer policy for staff artists is also responsible in making the programmes monotonous. The listeners of the region are compelled to listen same voices, same recitals and same compositions for a longer period, as most of these staff artists are stationed at one place till their retirement.

Merits and De-merits

Although, AIR has done a lot in improving the programme and technical quality of the classical music, there are still some constraints in the way of further improvements.

In order to improve the working of AIR, number of committees and study teams were set-up. Central Programme Advisory Committee (CPAC), the Central Advisory Board of Music (CABM) and the Music Audition Board (MAB), are the main which were set-up in fifties to advise the Minister on AIR matters. Programme Advisory Committees are also setup at all capital stations to advise about programmes. Most of the members of these committees are non-official.

Apart from the above regular committees, special committees and study groups were also setup to advise the government about the structure of broadcasting for better results. The Chanda Committee was setup in 1964, when Mrs. Gandhi became I&B Minister for a short period. In 1977, Janta Govt. constituted 'The Working Group on Autonomy of Akashvani and Doordarshan, called Verghese Committee. Staff Inspection Unit (SIU) and Parthasarthy Committee were also constituted for the purpose of re-structuring the setup of AIR. Earlier, there was a study team under the headship of Mehra Masani in 1967.[22]

These committees and study teams gave their findings and reports for improvements in the performance of AIR. How many of these recommendations were accepted by the Government is another question. The autonomous structure of AIR was very much suggested by the Chanda Committee in 1964 and it was mentioned that "It is not possible in the Indian context for a creative medium like broadcasting to flourish under a regiment (Sic) of departmental rules and regulations. It is only by an institutional change that AIR can be liberated from the present rigid financial and administrative procedures of Government."[23] Similarly, the Verghese Committee report was also submitted during the period of Janta Government, but nothing solid was done.

Some broadcasters and experts, who spent their whole life in this media, tried to suggest some measures for better working. Some observations made by these experts which are available in print, are quoted here.

Mr. G.C. Awasthy in Broadcasting in India stated: "A senior Government official once stated that administration means administration of personnel procedures for drawing salaries, TA, pension and leave rules etc. The unstated implication was that personnel are the same, no matter what they do, and therefore; administration means the same thing in all departments of the government. One had no doubt that he was voicing the views of majority of officials, and was giving expression to the practical philosophy of the Government of India. According to this view, an ICS or IAS officer is equally equipped to administer the armed forces or a cultural establishment. So applied, this philosophy makes a force of a service like broadcasting....Administration may be efficient in itself, and yet not quite favourable for creative work like broadcasting. Those who have been at the helm of affairs in AIR over the past decade may have known something about the administration of a district, but they did not understand the requirements of broadcasting. Only a person who has had actual experience of programme production will be in a position to keep administration from encroaching on the interests of the programmes."[24]

Commenting on the music audition system, Shri Awasthy wrote: "It soon became evident that the Music Audition Board was quite un-equal to the task of dealing with the large number of artists awaiting audition throughout the country. As the Board failed to meet sufficiently often, it was not unusual for a candidate to have to wait for two or three years before he or she qualified for broadcast."[25]

Commenting on recruitment policy, Mehra Masani stated; "AIR has been well aware that this method of recruitment has failed to give it the type of staff it requires but a Government department cannot opt out of the Government's machinery and methods of staff recruitment..... It demands a variety of professional experience and skill and a capacity for quick decision which can thrive only in an atmosphere of intellectual freedom."[26]

In fact, the most important factor for the poor programme quality is the low morale and poor wages of the staff. "...the standard of planning, production, and presentation of programmes depends on the standard of the junior staff. Their low wages, poor facilities and poor morale affect seriously the quality of programmes."[27] Particularly, in the case of music programmes, where creative skill is more important than the educational qualifications. Commenting on the administrative set-up Miss Masani stated; "the administrative and financial rules and procedures of government are quite unsuited to the needs of a broadcasting service. They do not permit the flexibility in budgeting and expenditure which is absolutely essential. Nor would they allow a redical reorganisation of the staffing pattern which would take into account the special needs of broadcasting."[28]

Narayan Menon, who was closely associated with the departments of mass communication and is a pioneer in this field, felt the need of boosting professional expertise. "Key decisions, policy decisions, which may change the whole course of development, progress are often taken by the people who have no professional expertise or involvement in mass communication... Can you imagine a broadcasting station in, say, Sweden which will have a Director who does not know Swedish? or a BBC station with a Director who does not know English? Or a French station with a non-French speaking Director? But we have Station Directors who do not know the local language. We not only have them, we have always had them, and what is more, we think that is right."[29]

Lord Windleshams in 'Broadcasting in a Free Society' (1980) expressed: Always there is a need to gaurd against over-rigid systems and towards spending too much time and care in attempting to define the indefinable. Instinct and judgement are invariable better guides then did tacticism. In broadcasting as elsewhere the bureaucracy will gain in strength, as well as in numbers unless positive steps are continuously taken to counter it."[30]

Comments of Shri Luthra on recruitment system: "The results of the steps already taken need to be assessed dispassionately after actual experience gained to see if the new system is working well or is creating undesirable tensions between different categories of staff when these should be working harmoniously, each man asked to do what he is best capable of."[31]

P.C. Chatterjee, former Director General of AIR observed that rigidity of rules never suited in programming: "The Director General cannot alter the scales of payment to musicians, actors, writers and other performers.....The Director Generals find themselves hamstrung because of standardised rules and procedures which operate uniformly in all departments of government. Little attention is paid to the peculiar needs of an organisation in terms of the functions it is required to perform."[32]

The audience of the radio programme is entirely different from other programmes like concerts, stage plays and cinema. "The singer on the concert platform, the actor on the stage, the lecturer on the rostrum are assured, at least to some extent, of a quiet and attentive audience, but the broadcast speaker, musician, or programme maker must project his material towards an audience already engaged in reading, writing, talking, eating, working, dressing or cooking. If he cannot succeed in gaining the listener's attention, his programmes must be judged as failures. Thus, in broadcasting, many accepted standards fail. "The ear divorced from the eye makes a new demand," wrote Mr. Jain. Hence the work of a broadcaster is more specialised and difficult as compared to the other means of the mass communication. And this difficult work can hardly be performed when art form is mixed up with politics. "A well known drama artist said that you can not mix art with politics and yet that is precisely what broadcasting has to do in India."[33]

As per K.S. Duggal, we are missing professionalism in radio; "What one misses in Akashvani and to an extent in Doordarshan is professionalism. There are few programme men who specialise in specific fields. This could be attributed to frequent inter-sectional and inter-station transfers. The only way to shake off mediocrity, with which the media are affected at present is to develop specialisation."[34]

M.S. Bedi, in his address as the President of Programme Staff Association, in the National Convention-1980; "The most saddening aspect is that Akashvani and Doordarshan are treated as any other department of the government. During the 44 years of its existence, the Government has failed to appreciate the creative, professional and highly specialised work in the broadcasting."[35]

Mr. Gopal Saxena, Director in Doordarshan expressed similar views; "A more sensitive, responsive and 'media-oriented' administration can certainly avoid and solve some of these problems. But present structural pattern and administrative procedures meant for radio and television, are hackneyed, out-moded, unrealistic and bureaucracy based."[36]

According to Melville De-Mellow, a renowned broadcaster; "Lack of taste-stimulation-ingenuity and excellence. In one word-lack of professionalism...The saddest part is that nobody seems to bother anymore. Shoddy programmes and performers are today accepted with the same apathy and resignation as soaring sugar prices—Power failures or dry taps; The lack of professionalism in AIR and TV is now SYSTEMETIC."[37]

Mr. De-Mellow also visualised communication gap between broadcaster and listener; "Listener' Research has been Radio's unwanted child and consequently has never been taken seriously. There is therefore no different to sloppy programmes."[38]

According to P.C. Chatterjee, we really need a consciously derrived communication policy at the National level; "A few years ago Mr. Gujral, who was then Minister for Information and Broadcasting, a person with a flair for language and himself a first rate communicator, said that 'what we need in AIR is a communication policy, not language policy. Since then, this had become a neat slogan which we have reeling off in parrot fashion whenever questions about language and communication arose."[39]

In addition to a well defined communication policy, we also need an improved staff structure to induce professionalism. However, what is needed by the Indian Broadcasting system can now easily be assessed, taking in view the comments and observations made above, by the experts and broadcasters.

References

1. G.C. Awasthy, *Broadcasting in India*, p. 191.
2. *Ibid.*, p. 193.
3. *Ibid.*
4. *Ibid.*
5. H.R. Luthra, *Indian Broadcasting*, p. 244.
6. *Ibid.*, p. 245.
7. H.R. Luthra, *Indian Broadcasting* and G.C. Awasthy's *Broadcasting in India*, p. 234 and 190.
8. *Ibid.*
9. H.R. Luthra, *Indian Broadcasting*, p. 281.
10. *Ibid.*, p. 282.
11. U.L. Baruah, *This is All India Radio*, p. 48.
12. *Ibid.*
13. Narayan Menon, *The Communication Revolution*, p. 32.
14. G.C. Awasthy, *Broadcasting in India*, p. 38.
15. H.R. Luthra, *Indian Broadcasting*, p. 283.
16. From the Fee scale chart of AIR.
17. U.L. Baruah, *This is All India Radio*, p. 59.
18. H.R. Luthra, *Indian Broadcasting*, p. 284.
19. Mehra Masani, *Broadcasting and the People*, p. 31.
20. H.R. Luthra, *Indian Broadcasting*, pp. 253, 254.
21. *Ibid.*
22. Edited from H.R. Luthra, *Indian Broadcasting* and G.C. Awasthy's *Broadcasting in India.*
23. *Ibid.*
24. G.C. Awasthy, *Broadcasting in India*, p. 190.
25. *Ibid.*, p. 191.
26. Mehra Masani, *Broadcasting and the People*, pp. 155, 33 and 169.
27. *Ibid.*
28. *Ibid.*

29. Narayan Menon in *The Communication Revolution*, pp. 33-34.
30. Lord Windleshams in *Broadcasting in free Society*, Quoted by Shri Luthra in *Indian Broadcasting*, p. 231.
31. H.R. Luthra, *Indian Broadcasting*, p. 243.
32. P.C. Chatterjee, *Broadcasting in India*, p. 192.
33. S.P. Jain, *The Art of Broadcasting*, p. 3.
34. K.S. Duggal, *Indian Broadcast Media*, Year Book.
35. M.S. Bedi, *Presidential Address,* PSA Convention, 1980.
36. Gopal Saxena, in an article, PSA Souvenir, 1980.
37. Melville De-Mellow in an article *Professionalism or Pay Packet*, Published in PSA Souvenir, 1980.
38. Melville De-Mellow in an article *Professional Excellence and All India Radio*, Published in PSA Souvenir, 1978.
39. P.C. Chatterjee, *Broadcasting in India*.

9

Broadcast of Indian Music from Foreign Broadcasting Organisation

(A brief survey)

Cultural Relations with Other Countries

Music is the best way of communication because it crosses the political and physical barriers which divide countries. The language is also not a hindrance to understand the meaning. The broadcasting made is easily accessible to the entire world to understand each other's culture. After the advent of broadcasting, many countries joined hands to exchange their programmes to enable the people of different countries to understand the culture and music of each other. These pacts of cultural exchange served useful purpose in popularising our music abroad.

In 1982, there were some 46 countries with which a pact of cultural exchange was signed. AIR is continuously supplying programmes to such countries where major part of the programme is music. It is also important to mention here that music does not have the limitations of language. In China, when D.V. Palusker presented a Bhajan, 'Thumak Chalat Ram Chandra' the copies of records sold were more than a lakh. The Chinese people did not understand the language but enjoyed musical part of it.

Countries with which pacts of cultural exchange have been signed are frequently broadcasting our programmes, where 50% of the programme contents are variety of music.

Role of Programme Exchange Unit of AIR

The role of Programme Exchange Unit of AIR, is not limited to exchange programmes between the stations of our country, it also supplies recordings of "Music, spokenword and other programme to about 150 countries and foreign broadcasting organisations under cultural exchange agreements and AIR's programme exchange agreements."[1] The programmes supplied to these countries contains 50 percent music programmes. Also, AIR brings out a quarterly bulletin giving details of radio programmes available for supply.

Role of External Services Division of AIR

Started in 1939, AIR now broadcasts in its External Services for a total of some 56 hours a day in twenty-five languages. The broadcasts in English are for 10 hours and in Urdu for 12 hours. The broadcast in English language are mainly beamed for Asia, Australia, New Zealand, East, West and North Africa, Britain and Western Europe, while the broadcast in Urdu are beamed for Pakistan. The other services are broadcast in Arabic, Baluchi, Bengali, Burmese, Cantonese, Dari, French, Gujrati, Hindi, Indonesian, Konkani, Mandarin, Nepali, Persian, Punjabi, Pushto, Russian, Sindhi, Simhaly, Swahili, Thai and Tibetan."[2]

Apart from the spoken work and news items, 50% time in the programmes is devoted to music. "Music is exclusively Indian music in the English and Indian languages services."[3] Apart from the Indian classical music, film music is popular in many countries in Europe, in the Arab world, Afganistan and in South East Asia."[4] "Besides popular music of the target area, Indian music of all types, light, folk and classical, with stress on orchestral and instrumental music, are broadcast with explanatory background."[5]

In addition to these services, the Programme Exchange unit of External Services does more than the services as the transcription and programmes exchange service; it keeps in constant touch with foreign missions to find out their requirements and regularly supplies them with programmes.[6]

The ESD familiarises foreign listeners with Indian music, thought and Indian culture. Whenever a good new programme is produced, copies are sent overseas.[7]

Nowadays, listeners in the Europe, Australia and New Zealand are showing keen interest in Indian Classical Music, particularly instrumental and orchestral.

Stations Around the World
(a brief survey)

It is beyond doubt that some 150 countries in the world broadcast Indian music of different kind under cultural exchange agreement and AIR's programme exchange agreement, but how much time is given to our programmes, is a matter of research.

Due to privatisation of broadcasting in American, European and several other countries, private owned radios have emerged like mushrooms, and number of such radios are in thousands. Hence it is very difficult to findout accurately, how many such radios broadcast Indian music. For example, in Canada, Indian music is broadcast only rarely from Canadian Broadcasting Corporation, but there are several private radios run by the private groups in Kingston, Vancouver, Edmonton and Toronto, whose programmes include East Indian Music.[8]

Similar situation prevails in England, Germany and America where considerable amount of Indians are living.

Out of my two years efforts, following details could be collected:

In England

(i) From BBC in Asian programmes on channel 4, Indian music is broadcast in Ethenic programmes almost daily.[9]

(ii) As per another information received, Indian music is not broadcast regularly from BBC (but occasionally) but there are other local stations broadcast Indian Music, mostly film music:

1.	LBC (London Broadcasting Co.)	One hour weekly every Sat.
2.	Greater London Radio	One hour weekly every Sat.

3. Sunrise Radio-London Regularly.[10]

In Canada

The Canadian Broadcasting Corporation does rarely broadcast Indian music, but following private local radios in Canada broadcast Indian music frequently or regularly:[11]

1. CFUV-FM, Student Union Bldg. PO Box 1700, Victoria, BC, V8W 2Y2.
2. CHIN, 637 College St. Toronto, ON, M6G 1B6.
3. CHIN-FM, 637 College St. Toronto, ON, M6G 1B6.
4. CIUT-FM, 9 St. George Street, Toronto, ON, M5S 2E8.
5. CJAM-FM, 401 Sunset Ave. Windsor, ON, N9B 3P4.
6. CJVB, 814 Richards St. Vancouver, BC, V6B 3A7.
7. CKJS, 520 Corydon Ave., Winnipeg, MB, R3L OP1.
8. CFMB, 35 rue York, Westmount, QC H3Z 2Z5
9. CFRC. Carruthers Hall, Queens University, Kingston, ON K7L 3N6
10. CFRC-FM Carruthers Hall Kingston, ON K7L 3N6
11. CHSR-FM Rm. 223, Student Union Bldg. P.O.Box 4400 Fredericton, NB E3B 5A3
12. CIAO 50 Kennedy Road South, Unit 20, Brampton, ON L6W 3R7
13. CKCU-FM Rm. 517. Unicentre, Carleton University, Ottawa, ON KlS 5B6
14. CKER 6005-103rd St. Edmonton, AB T6H 2H3
15. CKMS-FM 200 University Ave. W Waterloo ON N2L 3Gl.

In USA

Some private stations in San-Fransisco broadcast film records- occasionally, they broadcast Indian classical music.[12]

In USSR

Indian music is broadcast from Tashkand and Sumerkand regularly in their Urdu and Hindi services and people there are interested in Indian music. They also enquire from Indian visitors about the supply of gramophone records.[13]

In New Zealand

Wellington Access Radio, New Zealand, broadcasts North Indian Music (Hindustani) for 60 minutes per week since 1980. The listening of the programme is about 3% which constitute some 10,000 listeners in the area.[14]

In Netherland-Holland

Information received from Radio Netherland states that a weekly programme of Indian Music is broadcast for about half an hour contains 90% film music and.10% North Indian Classical Music. This programme was started in 1973 and still continues.

Another information received says that there are two local Hindustani Radio Stations in Amsterdam (i) Radio Jagte Raho (ii) Radio Sargam. Both Radio stations broadcast 12 hours Indian entertainment programmes which include Women programme, Children, Disco, Geets and Gazals and music of Pakistan. The languages of programmes are Hindi, Urdu, Punjabi and Surinami (mixture of Hindi and Urdu). The names of the popular artists are Dilip Roy, Usha Uthup, Alisha Chinoy, Annu Malik, Kishore, Lata, Rafi, Anupama, Pt. Somnath Sharma, Amit Kumar, Mannadey, Chandru Atma, Sudha Malhotra, A. Hariharan, etc.

These programmes include Geets, Gazals, Bhajans, and other light and light classical items. The opening and closing signature tunes are Pahadi Dhun (Instrumental tune).[15]

In Malasiya

Malasiya has a regular Tamil Service and broadcast South Indian Music as well as Hindustani. They invite or book on visit, artists from India.[16]

In Sri Lanka

We have been listening to Sri Lanka (earlier Ceylon) for a long period of time and in its commercial service Hindustani music is broadcast at 9:45 a.m. and 10:45 p.m. apart from commercial film records.

Even in its All Asia Service, number of chunks are alloted to Indian music like Geetanjali, Gaan Taranga, Swarga Swar, Gaan Sudha etc. which is broadcast almost daily. The Service is run in two transmissions (i) 6:00 a.m. to 10:00 a.m. (ii) and 6:00 p.m. to 11:00 p.m. Other chunks in these transmissions are Musical Miscellany and Night music, which include considerable amount of Indian classical music.[17]

In Fiji

From Govt. National Radio, regular service of Gramophone records is broadcast for Indians which includes variety of music.[18]

In Mauritius

Govt. Radio broadcast Indian Music regularly and invites artists from India. The service is supplied recorded music by AIR regularly.[19]

In Pakistan and Bangladesh

The music of Pakistan and Bangladesh is nothing but Hindustani music. The great artists like Gulam Ali, Menhdi Hasan, Nazakat Ali, Salamat Ali etc. are trained in purely Hindustani traditions and sing same ragas, thumri, gazals as sung in India. Runa Laila of Bangladesh belongs to the same category. Songs of Tagore and Nazurul Islam are broadcast frequently from Bangladesh.

Both countries were the part of India before partition and share same cultural heritage.[20]

SAARC Audio Visual Exchange

Nowadays (after formation of SAARC) the member countries of SAARC are frequently exchanging programmes and hence Indian Music is broadcast regularly in the member countries.[21]

Non-Align Countries

Members of the Non-Align groups are also exchanging programmes.[22]

In Phillipines

Govt. Radio rarely broadcast Indian Music but Radio Veritas broadcast Hindi Serial every alternative day which includes Indian music.[23]

Listening Abroad

So far the listening interest in these countries is concerned, it will be appropriate to mention that, it has not reached masses. However, a little interest has been induced and people in the world has started to understand richness of our music.

"It is foolish to think that Indian Music is listened in other countries in masses, but the listening and interest has increased, considerably.

Now you cannot think that a white man sitting side by side in the concert hall of classical music does not know anything about Indian Music.

There is small community, but they are real listeners of Indian Music. Now they are so accustomed that no artist can fool them."[24]

Western musicians are now taking keen interest in introducing Indian music to foreign audiences. 'Oliver Messiaen and Benjamin Britten; the indefatigable Yehudi Menuhin, who as long-time President of the Asian Music Circle in London has been most active in promoting a meeting of minds between Asian and Western musicians; Julian Bream, the classical guitar player (who has visited many parts of India and collaborated with Ali Akbar Khan, India's most famous contemporary player); Pierre Boulez, Larry Adler and Dave Brubeck, the jazz musician; and coming to the younger generation of popular music, George Harrison of the Beatles, who has most seriously undertaken a study of Indian philosophy as well as the music.'[25]

There are many of the most intelligent and musically experimental pop groups who have turned to India....Western media also played a significant role in popularising Indian music in the West. "Films, television and radio programmes (certainly in Britain) now introduce Indian music without a hair's being turned. This would have been inconceivable even ten years ago. My husband made one of the first television programmes on Indian Music in 1957; it was given a very late night showing on BBC television as being of minority interest."[26]

References

1. Publication Division, Ministry of I&B, *Mass Media in India*, 1981-83, p. 135.
2. P.C. Chetterjee, *Broadcasting in India*, pp. 149-150.
3. *Ibid.*
4. *Ibid.*
5. U.L. Baruah, *This is All India Radio,* pp. 94-95.
6. S.P. Jain, *The Art of Broadcasting,* p. 35.
7. *Ibid.*
8. A report from CBC dated 20-03-1989.
9. Interview with Shri P.V. Krishna Murthy, Ex DG TV, on 7-10-1990 at ISRO, Ahmedabad.
10. Letter from Dheeranjan Malve posted at BBC dt. 19-1-1989.
11. Letter from Douglas Ward, Director of Programming CBC Radio, Ottawa.
12. Interview with Shri P.V. Krishnamurthy, Ex DG TV, and at present Media consultant UNICEF on 7.10.90 at ISRO Ahmedabad.
13. *Ibid.*
14. Letter from Bala Thomson from Wellington dt. 2-11-1988.
15. Letter from Mr. Marrir Sarbroti from Amsterdam dt. 27-01-89.
16. Interview with Shri P.V. Krishnamurthy dt. 07-10-90.
17. Letter from Shri Sudhakarah dt 14-10-88.
18. Interview with Shri P.V. Krishnamurthy dt. 07-10-90.
19. *Ibid.*
20. Personal experience in broadcasting.
21. *Ibid.*
22. *Ibid.*
23. Interview with Father Lucas, Owner of Local Radio in Phillipines on 07-10-90 at ISRO, Ahmedabad during Local Radio Workshop.
24. Interview with Shri P.V. Krishna Muthry, Ex DG TV and Media Consultant UNICEF on 07-10-90 at ISRO Ahmedabad.
25. Peggy Holroyde, *Indian Music, A Vast Ocean of Promise*, pp. 27-28.
26. *Ibid.*

10

The New Patron of Hindustani Music

STUDY OF QUALITATIVE AND QUANTITATIVE CHANGES DUE TO THE FACTORS OF TOTAL EXPOSURE, EFFECTIVENESS AND IMPACT OF THE MEDIA (RADIO)

Changing Phases

From its journey from the ancient time to modern age, Indian music has passed through various changing phases in terms of its quality and quantity both. The styles (Shaily) and varieties have varied widely due to different political, social and economic factors. Although, every phase has given a new dimension, traditional concept and identity is still maintained.

Considering various phases from Vedic period to modern age, the changes in traditions, which radio brought were unique, different and quick. It was a co-incident that radio emerged at a time when the Hindustani music was passing through strain and stress and was in search of new Patron.[1]

The New Patron

Mr. J.C. Mathur in *Aspects of Indian Music* writes, "when radio came on the Indian scene in thirties in this country, music was already on the look out for new patronage."[2]

He further wrote "As a result of the new economic impact the princes and landlords gradually ceased to be the patrons of music. The theatre had been unceremoniously jettisoned by cinema. Though the early films made use of classical melodies, it was clear from the very beginning that their new form of entertainment would not have much use of traditional and classical music, and would depend upon other devices for enlivening its presentation. However, the gramophone continued. Although, the long playing record was still far off, old masters continued to derive some income, but less satisfaction, from the brief recordings they were able to give. In such a situation, it was doubtful whether high class Indian music could survive as a form of art and entertainment. It was then that the radio came to the scene with its offer of opportunities to both, the old masters and promising young artists. Musicians could now give freer play to their art and reach the homes of the people in their hours of leisure. Little wonder that this new found patronage brought a sense of liberation to artists."[3]

The Indian music hence found new patron of culture, as per Mehra Masani: "It has portrayed popular culture which other agencies could not transmit."[4]

"All India Radio, as a patron of music, presents the cultural heritage of India. It seeks to bring together and to encourage mutual understanding of the different forms of music, like classical, semi-classical, light and folk music"[5] wrote S.P. Jain.

According to P.C. Chatterjee, former DG, AIR, "During British period, princely houses provided the patronage under which classical music flourished. Since 1947, AIR had done a great deal to fill the gap arising from the removal of the princes from the political scene."[6]

Even during the period of princely patronage, musicians did not enjoy freedom and popularity as they enjoyed from radio. According to Luthra, who slightly differ from the earlier statements: "It has been claimed sometimes that AIR took the place of princes as patrons of muisc when the old order of Rajas and Nawabs yielded place in 1947, to the new democratic setup on the attainment of Independence. This is not the whole truth because except for certain enlightened rulers who were themselves keen on music and did much to encourage it, most of their

Highnesses were interested in other forms of entertainment. Also, not many musicians, except perhaps some outstanding ones enjoyed freedom from pecuniary wants."[7]

This statement of Mr. Luthra, is true to a great extent. Patronage and freedom provided by All India Radio is different and better if compared with the period of Princes and rulers where musical activities were limited to the courts only. The role of AIR in popularising classical music has been carried out in much broader sense and has not been measured so far as per Chatterjee; *"This thesis of AIR inheriting the mantle of patron has not been documented by sociological research and the influence of radio on classical music has not been assessed."*[8]

From Darbars to Masses

The very first thing done by Radio has to arrange concerts of the great artists in open, out of courts of the native princes. Before radio, the concerts were confined to walled areas of Mahals and villas of rulers with limited audience comprising of ruling class. The artists who could not get such patronage were roaming on streets or singing and dancing in Kothas-dancing and singing cells, which in turn were again patronised by urban rich leaving no chance for common man.

Commenting on AIR's cultural role in popularising classical music, H.K.L.Bhagat, the then Minister of I&B said 'Classical music is no longer the preserve of the previleged few as radio has taken to every home. AIR has played no small role in encouraging old and traditional music of India. Also, its light music output was both significant and substantial."[9]

Where print media is important in bringing socio-political revolutions, radio has played an important role in bringing 'cultural revolution'. Radio, in the last four decades, has been able to assert certain traditions in the field of performing art. The old traditions were quickly replaced by new ones and limitations of time and duration forced artists to change their attitude, habits and traditions.

Here, in this chapter, these aspects, of changing traditions, will be discussed in detail touching almost every aspect. There is nothing on record, nor any survey has so far been conducted to study the effects. The conclusions are based on the material available, personal experiences and surveys, and some interview with the artists, musicians and broadcasters, who are deeply associated with the electronic media and performing art. In the earlier chapters, quantitative aspects were discussed in detail, here, survey is based on qualitative factors.

Secrets Disclosed

The artists and outstanding musicians did not come out of the Darbars or Kothas even after the regular broadcasts were started in India, because they were zealous gaurdians of their art and were not ready to reveal the peculiarities and styles of their performance which they have learnt from their Ustad of particular School (Gharana). The aspirants of one school were not allowed to adopt the styles of other school even remotely, and belonging to a school was a matter of pride and no disciple dared to disobey. This rigidity created problems in introducing the artists to masses. The great masters were not readily agreeable to perform over radio. The main reason was the fear of disclosure of style because each one felt superior to other.

"There were, however, few exceptions, but very rare indeed, and even these would not have occurred if some of the sensitive souls had been handled with great care, or if the artists themselves had not laid down certain conditions which AIR could not possibly agree to," wrote Luthra, "One artist insisted that he be paid just one rupee more than anyone else."[10]

However, situation improved when audition and gradation system was introduced, but Secrets ultimately disclosed to the public.

Gharanas (Schools) and Broadcasting

With the introduction of new audition system in 1952, the old tradition of schools (Gharanas) collapsed. Selection by MAB is being made purely on the basis of the performance and Gharana is not a matter of consideration for the purpose of selection of artist. Nowadays, number of new styles are emerging where peculiarities of different Gharanas are mixed. This is because of the exposure of different kind of music from the media. Pt. Ravi Shanker, in an interview in a TV programme telecast on 8-5-1990- 'Khayal': "Different styles are mixed up as the artists are more exposed to Media."[11]

The interviews with other artists reveal that the artists are now adopting various styles of playing and singing mixingup peculiarities of different schools. Of course, there is no harm in adopting good styles of other school. Lot of innovation has been done in this field and rigid attitude of the masters is fadingout.

Artists interviewed in this regard are of the same opinion and they do not think any wrong in it. This is also one of the greatest achievement of radio.

The new audition system of AIR brought many other new changes in the attitude of the artists. First time in the history, the artists were united to fight against the new policies of AIR in 1952 forgetting the differences between the various Gharanas. The artists of various schools first time came nearer. Though, most of artists belong to some Gharana or the other, but they are not so rigid as they were earlier. A common listener is hardly aware about the school to which artist belongs, he is only concerned with the quality of performance.

Other Impacts

AIR has, directly or indirectly, influenced the growth of Indian classical music. With the invention of gramophone records the pattern of singing and playing was influenced only upto a limited extent, i.e. the duration of performance. The gramophone records of old masters for three minutes duration are still popular and now dubbed in LP records. But AIR as a whole, influenced the patterns in so many ways, such as time and duration, strict punctuality, softness in the voice and habit of singing without audience etc.

Binding of Time and Duration

Earlier, our great masters and Ustads were in a habit of singing or playing for long hours without any binding of time and duration. It was also at the will of the artist to choose the *raga* at the nick of time and audience was not aware till the opening of the programme, which *raga* Ustad will sing. The programmes were arranged mostly in the form of concerts and sometimes these concerts continued till next morning. The response and appreciation of the audience sustained the mood of the artist to continue for hours.

This was just not possible on radio. In the beginning, when artists were invited by radio, they refused to accept any condition of time and duration. The programmes in those days were broadcast live and the artist was first briefed to start his performance after the opening announcements and was asked to windup few seconds before the stipulated period, leaving time for closing announcements, as AIR always observed strict punctuality. It was not possible to over carry. News or important broadcasts must adhere to schedule. If the artist forgot to conclude, the programme had to be fadedout under such compulsions.

The centuries old traditions with our old masters was to sing whatever they liked without any limit of time. However, AIR has been able to influence this habit and even top ranking artists agreed to give their performance for the duration ranging from 3 minutes to 90 minutes as required by AIR for its fixed chuncks.

This has, no doubt, altered the pattern of recitals and a style, different from stage performance. The artists tried to accommodate all his styles and peculiarities he learnt from his master within the prescribed time limit. There are some recordings of our great masters like Pt. Ravi Shanker, Pt. D.V. Palusker, Abdul Karim Khan Sahed and others, in which the artists had tried to accommodate all their patterns like Aalap, Jod, Bilambit, Drut Layas and Jhala, within three minutes duration.

According to a well-known performing artist, the continuity of the recital is maintained by the performer as he is interested in showing his professional skill within the prescribed time limit, while in concerts, the artist allows the accompanists (like Tabla, Harmonium or Sarangi) to perform in between his recital while he relaxes a bit during performance, because there is no such time limit on the stage. On the contrary, on radio, artist plans his performance in such a way, that all his work is beautifully adjusted in a given period of time. This is done by choosing selected styles he prefers to play on radio.

However, these minor differences in performance can hardly be noticed by an ordinary listener, but the experts and musicologists very much observe this change. The artists now are also in a habit of playing differently on stage from radio. They are well conversant with the rules of stage and radio. They have to pay extra care while performing on radio as listener, they know, is not bound to listen the programme as in the case of concert hall, where the audience is devoting his extra time and money for attending concert. The artist is very much aware that if the programme is not attractive, a listener may switch-off or tune-over to other station.[12]

Although, these observations are minute, but constitute an important change in the patterns of singing and playing. Even, stage programmes are now arranged in such a way that time limit and punctuality is maintained. However, the rules are not strictly followed as in radio, where the duration is measured in seconds.

Radio has started its own traditions which influenced the styles, behaviour and the old practices, popular for centuries, in the musical society.

Punctuality

The performance of any artist in those days very much depended on the mood of the artist, and punctuality was not a binding for them. The professionals too were little slow especially those among the top musicians.

In radio, "there was a discipline of time because with the programmes having to be published in advance, they had to observe strict punctuality to which they were not used."[13] However, AIR forced them to be punctual. On so many occasions when the artist did not turn-up for broadcast as per schedule, the item was substituted and as a punishment, the artist was banned for certain period.

AIR reserve the right to ban any artist who defaults without any solid reason. This happened even in the case of popular musicians. As soon as more and more artists were attracted to AIR, there was no fear of interruption in broadcast. Moreover, there was sufficient recorded material to substitute the scheduled programme. To honour the commitment to the listeners, it was necessary for AIR to see that the programme scheduled and published should go on air at any cost except for the reasons beyond control. When few artists started defaulting, the only alternative with the AIR left was to ban their broadcast. This practice of AIR was sometimes criticized, but taking in view the commitment to the people, calculated in millions, steps taken by AIR were legitimate.

However, situation improved in the course of time and artists became punctual not only for AIR programmes but also in their outside engagements.

Influence on Tonal Quality

Sarangadeva, great luminary said that following are considered by the great musicians and musicologists as attributes of a good voice—*richness, flexibility, steadiness and smoothness.*[14] Particularly for classical singing, these qualities are not only important but also essential. "In addition to these qualities, the voice must be able to execute all types of graces or ornaments and tone colours or dynamics to sing the classical music of to-day which has been enriched and enlarged by the great composers of the past. Without these qualities, a singer cannot shine in the branch of Indian classical music."[15]

Much more has been said about the qualities of voice and most important in the caste of classical music is that "every singer should keep his voice 'sweet' and melodious to exhibit his musical skill."[16]

Singing is interconnected not only with the whole physical organisation of the body, but also with feeling, attitude, intellect and intuition. The physiological mechanism 'Voice' is controlled more by the psychological part 'will'.

Even if, intellect and intuition of the above psychological factors are same, the feelings and attitude will definitely change when a singer is performing at a new or different place or other than stage, more clearly, in the studios where the conditions are different from those present in the concert halls, where huge audience is present for response and appreciation. The audience appreciation creates different feeling and attitude than the performance in the airconditioned and soundproof studios, sitting alone, without response.

That is why, there is difference in the broadcasts of studio recordings and programmes recorded in the concerts before invited audience. One can easily differentiate between two programmes. To create liveliness, AIR also arranges such concerts periodically where recordings are broadcast later

There is lot of difference noticed in the tonal quality of the performances after the improvements in the technical equipments used in broadcasting, both in vocal and instrumental recitals. Old recordings of our great masters are the best example in this regard. The recordings of Ustad Faiyyaz Khan, Ustad Abdul Karim Khan etc. contain more loudness and harshness in vocal. Similarly, old recordings of Ustad Allauddin Khan and Ustad Hafiz Ali Khan do not contain good tonal quality. While at present, singers use soft and melodious voices.[17]

In fact, there should be proper balance between the loudness and sweetness, which is not, in some cases seen in the past recordings, and main reason behind this was that old masters were habitual to sing in the concerts where microphones and loudspeakers were not available in those old days and adequate loundness was necessary to provide listening to the last row of the audience. This had ultimately, affected the tonal quality of their performance.

This trend continued in the early days of broadcasting. With the introduction of modern technology, tonal quality has considerably improved, and tremendous change in the output has been noticed. After the introduction of FM and qraplic equilizers, revolutionary changes has been observed in the tonal quality.

From Neglect to Respect

The greatest achievement of AIR has been to provide status to the art form and its artists which was mostly neglected in the society for different social factors.

It has been mentioned earlier in this work and is a well known fact, that the music was not respected in the society even after Independence. It was an unfortunate state of affair created during the British period. However, we should be thankful to dancing and singing professionals for preserving the treasury of this art, and keeping it alive during the days of sufferings. Due to them only, upto a certain extent, this art form is still alive. But public life of these dancing and singing girls was not respected in the middle and lower class families. And this was the reason, music was not respected in the society.

When AIR started broadcasting programmes of these Baijis (re-named as Devis), the thinking of the society started changing in this regard.

After the assumption of charge by Dr. Keskar as Minister of I&B, such broadcasts became frequent, and very soon, these Devis acquired the status of eminent artists and given chance in the National programmes. Later, number of such artists were awarded Padma Shri, and AIR got credit for this achievement.

Today, situation is different and music and its artists are very much respected in the society. And this was done by the Radio by its power to mould the taste and psyche of the listening public.

Popularity among Laymen and Youth

'Classical Music' as said by Ustad Vilayat Khan, 'was', 'is' and 'will' be preserved by the few intellectuals; 'which means, it will never interest common man. This is not whole truth now. It is true, that it will take time, when total population will be interested in the classical music, but the efforts and experiments carried out in the past by AIR have created interest in the common man and it can be verified from the figures of participants of AIR Music Competitions and Youth Programmes:

AIR Music Competition

AIR arranges annual music competition for Hindustani and Karnatak music, both, instrumental and vocal, in which young artists from the age group of 16 to 24 are invited, and over 2000 young artists participate in AIR Annual Music Competition. AIR music competition was started in mid seventies which became extremely popular among youth, and more than a lakh artists have so far participated in the last 20 years. The winners of the competition are awarded B grade by AIR without any audition. Such competitions were arranged by AIR earlier but a set pattern was introduced at a later date.

Annual music competitions are conducted at all AIR stations to encourage and locate young artists. This has diverted the interest of our youth from Western to Indian classical music.

Yuvwani Programme

An exclusive channel 'Yuvwani' was introduced on 21st July, 1969. The format of this programme was to cater the listening needs and participation of younger generation. There are separate channels of this programme at Delhi, Hyderabad,

Calcutta and Srinagar and other originating stations broadcast this programme for an hour or so, daily, in addition to other variety programmes.

In addition to other variety programmes, young artists of classical music are given chance frequently. The programme is very much popular among youth and number of young artists of classical music are increasing day by day.

The introduction of classical music in this programme has tremendous effect on younger generation and students. There are approximately 10,000 young artists who are participating in AIR's youth programme particularly in classical music. The students who, earlier were interested only in film music have now started paying respect to our traditional art form. Classical music concerts, which were earlier hooted by the students, are now frequently attended by the youth.

Role of Vividh Bharati

In 1957, when Vividh Bharati service was introduced, it was very much felt that it is not possible to change the taste of the masses with the twinkling of eye. It is a time bound process. Vividh Bharati service not only attracted listeners, but also played a vital role in moulding the taste of the listeners from light and film music to classical music. It is generally understood that Vividh Bharati Service broadcasts only for the light listeners and most of the time is devoted for film music. In this context, it is important to mention that entire film music is not cheap and vulgar, on the contrary, some of the film songs are based on the classical *ragas* and are of a high standard. Just because of few vulgar songs, whole film music cannot be discarded. For example, songs of musical hit films like *Basant Bahar, Baiju Bavra,* etc. were composed on *ragas* of classical music. Few of the *ragas* are recognised by the film songs by a common man. We cannot forget pioneering efforts of our great playback singers and music directors. K.L. Sahgal, Jaddan Bai, Jutika Roy, K.C. Day, Pankaj Mallik, and even Lata, Asha, Rafi and others, had their training in purely Indian traditions and were classical singers in their early days. Similarly our great music directors, like Naushad, Khayyam, Gulam Mohammed, Shanker Jaikishan etc. are great pioneers of Indian classical music and their tunes in films are based on classical *ragas*.

Vividh Bharati film music programmes at least have created interest of the common man towards music and later towards our classical music also. A number of listeners came to know about the names and tunes of popular *ragas* only through listening to film songs. *Raga Malkaus* is popular among the light listeners with the popularity of film song *'Man Tarasat Hari Darshan Ko Aaj'* sung by Rafi for film *Baiju Bavra*. Similarly, some other songs from musical hit film like *Basant Bahar, Shri 420, Aag, Chitralekha* etc. are extremely popular.

Classical Music through Film Music

To popularise classical music among common listeners, Vividh Bharati did a successful experiment by introducing film music in music lesson programme. Three to four minutes cut of classical music is played alongwith a popular film song based on that *raga*. This was liked by listener. The programme is broadcast daily. This *Sangeet Sarita* programme is extremely popular and is able to popularise classical music among film music listeners. Popularity of this programme has already been discussed in earlier chapter. A personal survey reveals that most of the beginners and students of classical music were influenced by this programme and started learning classical music. Few of them are still regular listeners of this programme.[18]

Music can never be cheap and vulgar as it was understood in 1952. The broadcast of film music through Vividh Bharati has played an indirect role in popularising classical music. The film music, in the first instance introduced the masses to the music. Popular film songs, made it easy to a layman to understand the 'term' music. A good deal of popular film songs, based on the *'Ragas'* were able to convince the laymen that good music will always be appreciated by all classes of society, and this was the first step to understand classical music. The film songs broadcast from Vividh Bharati, brought the laymen nearer to classical music which was the easiest way to understand *raga*.

I do not say that listening of film songs and *'Sangeet Sarita'* produced artists, but it has, indirectly created interest towards music, and at least produced listeners. Thus Vividh Bharati played an outstanding role in popularising classical music through film music.

Sangeet Sarita Programme

Vividh Bharati has maximum listening (upto the extent of 80%) both in rural and urban population. *Sangeet Sarita* programme was introduced in 1973 attracted millions of listeners from all corners of the country and average listening is around 20%. The listening figures also indicate that the maximum listening of this programme is among the youth of the middle and higher income groups.

Number of Artists and Listeners of Classical Music

Apart from the young artists participating in AIR's Annual Music Competition (about 2000 each year) and in Yuvwani programme (approximately 10,000) there are over 27,000 classical music artists of Hindustani and over 30,000 artists of Karnatak music on the approved list of AIR, and there are a lot more who appear in audition every year and do not qualify. "It goes without saying that AIR to-day is the biggest patron of Indian Classical Music."

So far the number of listeners are concerned, if calculated at the rate of 19% listening (All India Listening figures of classical music), in 95 millions (now the number has gone to more than 100 millions) radio sets, the total number of regular listeners comes to 18.05 millions.

Cultural Ambassador

The broadcast of Indian music has already been discussed in ealier chapter, where several countries of the world more or less broadcast our music. Still, our programmes of classical music are listened in other countries and our National Programme of Music is extremely popular in other countries and is said to be the *Cultural Ambassador* of our country.

The future of Indian classical music is now bright under the patronage of Radio. There are millions of listeners increasing day by day, and with the introduction of new project of 'Local Radio', National Channel and Stereo broadcasting, it is for sure, that the growth in this field will be faster than ever, when the radio will reach almost every home.

References

1. Dr. A.K. Banerjee, *Changing Phases*, Research Paper-for detail study.

2. J.C. Mathur in *Aspects of Indian Music,* quoted by U.L. Baruah in *This is All India Radio*, p. 130.
3. J.C. Mathur in *Aspects of Indian Music*, quoted by U.L. Baruah in *This is All India Radio*, pp. 130-131.
4. Mehra Masani, *Broadcasting and the People*, p. 4.
5. S.P. Jain, *The Art of Broadcasting*, p. 24.
6. P.C. Chatterjee, *Broadcasting in India*, p. 142.
7. H.R. Luthra, *Indian Broadcasting*, p. 300.
8. *Ibid.*
9. Speech by Mr. H.K.L. Bhagat, as Minister for I&B on 18th March, 1988 inaugurating AIR, Delhi Stereo Service.
10. H.R. Luthra, *Indian Broadcasting*, p. 300.
11. Pt. Ravi Shanker in a TV Programme telecast on 8-5-1990 'Khayal.'
12. Based on personal experience and interviews with artists.
13. H.R. Luthra, *Indian Broadcasting*, p. 299.
14. S.K.A. Durga, *Voice Culture*, p. 73.
15. *Ibid.*
16. *Ibid.*, p. 5.
17. From personal listening in AIR.
18. Analysis of survey report (personal).

11

Present Situation

Total Coverage

Total Radio Stations

At present, (till this chapter is written) total number of radio stations is 148 including 47 local stations, covering almost entire population of the country, with its MW-SW and FM transmitters.[1] Commercial Broadcasting Service is also running from 29 MW transmitters carrying Vividh Bharati Service. In addition, External Services Division is broadcasting programmes in 25 languages round the clock through its 16 High power transmitters.

Local Radio

The new concept of Local Radio was emerged during the Sixth Plan period, but could only be materialised during Seventh Plan when commissioning of 74 Local Radios was planned. Only 8 such stations could start working by the end of the Seventh Plan. Most of the other stations are ready and awaiting inauguration. By 1993 there were 47 stations working.

It is also proposed that by the end of Eighth Plan, the total number of radio stations will be raised to 210.[2]

Earlier, it was proposed that by the end of Eighth Plan, each linguistic zone will be provided with a Local Radio, when at least each district will have one radio station, but taking in view the progress, it may take more time in future.

The programme pattern of these local stations is different from those, working at Regional and National levels. The programmes of these stations are flexible, need based and local talent is involved, who otherwise were unable to participate in the communication process. It will be a two way communication and programmes will be area specific and field based. These stations will function as a mouth-piece of local community and will reflect and enrich its life and artistic expressions.

The main objective of the local radio is to introduce local talent. There is a provision to give chance to junior and unauditioned artists, who could not pass the test of Audition Board due to strict audition rules. Hence the local artists of classical music are able to give their performance over local radio of their area. *Music lovers are thrilled because of its FM transmission, when they listen disturbance free and clear programme.*

National Channel

National Channel has become operative with effect from 19th May, 1988, through its 1000 KW MW transmitter at Nagpur, (Studios at Jawaharlal Nehru Stadium, New Delhi). Service is broadcasting its programmes from 6.55p.m. to 6-10a.m. (over night service) next day and quality programmes of national importance are broadcast.

In addition to Spoken word programmes, major part of programmes contains music, which includes classical music (Hindustani and Karnatak) at 1-30a.m. and 4a.m., Devotional Music at 5a.m. and Western Music at 11-15p.m.[3] Programmes broadcast are of high quality and stations are also contributing their best productions to this service. The service will be further extended to cover whole country.

AIR network can now be divided into three segments: (i) National, (ii) Regional, and (iii) Local, which is generally called three tier service.

Stereo Broadcast for Music

Stereo Music Service has been inaugurated at AIR Delhi on 18th March, 1988. This is another landmark in the history of broadcasting. Although, we are late but now joined the elite band of broadcasting organisations, already using such type of advanced and sophisticated technology. This will provide high quality of music software for listeners of music programme.[4]

Stereo sounds are much more natural and fascinating because it has a quality of creating impression about the spatial distribution of various sound sources. In contrast with the mono sound where every thing appears to originate from a point source, stereo can simulate locations of different performers in the space between two loud speakers.

In future, all the four metropolitan cities will be provided with this service, however it is a dream for a common man in near future.

At present, Delhi is broadcasting music from this service daily at 9-30 p.m. on its FM channel on 107.1 Mega Htz.[5]

Total Hours of Broadcast (Music Programmes)

Figures upto 1982 are available when 86 radio stations were working. The total programme broadcast during this year was for 5,72,329 hours out of which 1,55,869 hours were devoted to music and 1,40,675 hours were taken by Vividh Bharati Service. Total broadcast of classical music was 52,143 hours in the year through 86 radio stations. Now number of radio stations have gone up by 148, it is calculated that the total broadcast hours of classical music must have crossed 60,000.

Hence 164 hours of classical music per day is being broadcast for 18.05 millions of listeners. No other service can do it.[6]

Technical Facilities (in Brief)

There have been lot of improvements in the technical facilities in the course of years, but if compared with those available in the developed and even few of underdeveloped countries, we are lagging behind the time.

The most important factor in this context is the radiation power of our transmitters. From day to day experience, one can easily observe that the programmes of AIR are hardly audiable on the shortwave band, while the programmes of other countries are clearly received. The power of our transmitters is so weak that the reception in our own country is poor. What is available for the listeners today is the regional service or Vividh Bharati.

A comparative study in 1982 reveals that we have to do a lot in this field. At present we have got 16 High Power Transmitters for our external service with the following strength:-

10 KW SW	One	Delhi
20 KW SW	One	Delhi
50 KW SW	Two	Delhi
100 KW SW	Seven	Delhi, Bombay and Madras.
250 KW SW	Two	Aligarh
100 KW SW	One	Jullundhur
1000 KW MW	Two	Calcutta and Rajkot.

"As against only two short wave transmitters of 200 KW or above, Radio Mascow has 63, Voice of America 58, BBC 26, Federal Republic of Germany 19, Radio France 8 and Radio Australia 4. Our 1000 KW MW transmitter has a fairly good reach during the night though it is vitiated often by heavy interference, but during the day, this cannot be heard clearly beyond 500 miles or so."[7]

Thanks to ASIAD-82 held in Delhi when a lot of new equipments were imported and later distributed to some stations, but could not fulfil the total requirements. Our Bharat Electronics Limited is also manufacturing new equipments to cope with the requirements of the expansion. Now old transmitters are being replaced and power of some of them is being increased during the 7th and 8th Plan. Most of the projects are under installation.

Facilities to Artists

The facilities to the artists have already been discussed in detail in earlier chapters, and there is not much change in the course of time.

As already stated, radio is not a good pay master, but name and fame which is earned by the artists through radio performances is enough to establish their respect and living. Most of the top ranking artists today were first introduced by the radio and became famous. In early days, it was a matter of pride to become radio artist.

The regular artists of AIR are availing better facilities and security and their service became pensionable. On the contrary, future of the casual artists is not that much secured. They still deserve more from the department.

Listeners Opinion

Suggestions and reactions from the listeners are always invited by AIR through their letters and Audience Research Unit conducting special surveys frequently for the purpose of feed-back from listeners. However "for any valid evaluation of the quality of programmes and the success of any production techniques adopted, the broadcaster, it is recognised, must rely on his own professional judgement and that of expert critics outside."[8]

Number of letters received by AIR has already been discussed in earlier chapters and it is very difficult to know real opinion of the listeners through surveys and analysis of letters, due to their limitations as sources of constructive criticism, but these can be useful in assessing the size of the audience for different types of programmes, the suitability of hours of broadcast and ascertaining general viewing and listening habits of the people.[9]

However, listeners opinion is always taken into consideration in the process of programme production but opinion of the broadcaster and the expert is always the best, because the producer knows his listener better.

Moreover, media has its own responsibility. It cannot always fulfil the demands of the majority of the listeners. It is also the duty of the media to broadcast standard programmes suitably,moulding the taste of listeners, which AIR is doing well.

"In the society like ours, the responsibility of the audience cannot be fulfilled only by providing the type of entertainment most listeners ask for. It is the social responsibility of the broadcasting organisation to interpret the results of audience research in relation to its other responsibilities of inform and educate its listeners, and to cultivate their taste for good entertainment."[10]

It is very difficult in our society to evaluate exact point of view of the listeners as they are not organised as in the case of developed countries. "In some countries Listeners' Councils have played a very important role in influencing the programme policies of the broadcasting service. In Britain, there is a Viewers' and Listeners' Association and a Radio and TV Committee consisting of writers and academies. Besides, the National

Council for Women, the National Institute of Adult Education, and others also exert pressure on one or other field of programme activity."[11]

So far the listening of classical music in India is concerned, the listener opinion is always positive, and healthy criticism is always taken into consideration while planning the programmes in addition to experts' opinion.

References

1. Latest report from year book (I&B) 1993.
2. H.K.L. Bhagat, Minister of I&B, reported by *Daily Alok* (Hindi) dt. 21-8-1988.
3. *Schedule of National Programmes,* Jan. to March, 1990.
4. *Daily M.P. Chronical* 19th March, 1988, publishing Inaugural speech of I&B Minister.
5. *Ibid.*
6. Calculated from tables (Appendix).
7. H.R. Luthra, *Indian Broadcasting*, p. 221.
8. *Ibid.*, p. 460.
9. *Ibid.*
10. Mehra Masani, *Broadcasting and the People,* pp. 140 and 143.
11. *Ibid.*

12

Impact of Telecasting on Broadcasting

(Listening of Classical Music)

Brief History

Although, the experiments on television started in 1924, the quality improved only after continuous efforts of about 12 years. "On 2nd November, 1936, BBC started telecasting programmes on experimental basis, when there were only 300 TV sets. Due to World War II, suddenly on Ist September, 1939, BBC television closed down and did not reopen till June, 7,1946."[1]

In India

In India an experimental television service started much later on September, 15, 1959, in Delhi only. We were late. "While radio in India made beginning, although a modest one, within a couple of years of its start in America, England and elsewhere in Europe, there was a big time lag in television."[2]

The progress of television in India was not as fast as that of radio. "It was a one hour service (twice a week on Tuesday and Friday evening) of which 40 mts were devoted to studio based programmes of social education intended for community centres and 20 minutes were given to filed entertainment material."[3]

At that time there were no private TV sets and sets were provided to 21 community centres in and around Delhi.

Except launching an Educational project in 1969 on regular basis, not much progress was made till 1972 when Bombay station started. In 1973, Srinagar Kendra was opened. Subsequently TV centres were setup in Calcutta, Madras, Lucknow, Amritsar, Jullundhur and relay transmitters at Mussoorie (for Delhi), Pune (for Bombay), Kanpur (for Lucknow) and Bangalore (for Madras and Bombay).[4]

The story remained almost same till 1982 when colour TV was introduced and Asian Games, 1982 were given a fuller coverage on National network. Low Power transmitters were also installed to relay National and network programmes. OB vans, Editing equipments, Cameras, Visual TBCS, etc. were imported in addition to Low Power transmitters. It was planned to instal one LPT in each distt. to give full coverage and number of such transmitters has gone beyond 400 till now.

However, TV expansion plan has been delayed considerable in India. Even in Pakistan, the progress was faster and colour TV started right from the beginning in 1964. Why we lagged behind? answered Mr. Luthra, "It must be recalled here that the delay in starting TV in India was because the general thinking of a succession of Finance Ministers was that television was only a status symbol, with very limited utility, and therefore not deserving any special priority in allocation of money needed by a poor country for other more pressing needs, especially of vast majority in village."[5]

It was never thought that the socio-economic development is directly related with the progress in the filed of mass communication.

Still coverage of Television is limited in so many ways and is not at present a serious rival to Radio. The various aspects are discussed in detail to prove the superiority of radio over TV.

Comparative Study

Availability

The availability of television sets is still not satisfactory as compared to the availability of radio sets. According to figures put out by Electronic Commission in 1988 the total number of TV sets was estimated at 12 millions as against over 60 millions radio sets. (According to latest figures the number of radio sets is estimated to 95 millions). "When one turns to the geographic distribution of television, one finds that some seven millions, that is over half are located in the cities of Delhi and Bombay. The remaining are to be found mainly in Calcultta and Madras with a sprinkling in the rest of the country."[6]

This shows that villagers or say common man is still left out with the availability of TV. On the other hand, radio set is available in the remote areas. The availability thus calculated is TV for 90 people as against the radio for 9 persons.

Size of the Audience

It is estimated that TV is covering about 70 percent of the population. However, the real size of the audience is far far less due to the reason that programmes of the Doordarshan are telecast only in two major languages, Hindi and English. The size of the TV audience is further reduced to this factor. "The fact is that the bulk of Doordarshan's programmes are presented in Hindi and English. Over all 39 percent of programmes are Hindi, 28 percent English, Tamil gets 11 percent and Marathi 5 percent. What other languages get is negligible. At the Madras centre, 40 percent of programmes are in Tamil, 24 percent in Hindi and 23 percent in English. No other regional language is so favoured. Bengali in Calcutta is used in only 25 percent of programmes, which is how Marathi fares in Bombay."[7]

Distance Covered

Television programmes are telecast on FM frequency which covers very small area. A 10 KW TV transmitter covers only 50 to 60 kms. radius. While a SW radio transmitter of the same strength covers almost entire state and some times entire country. LPT of television covers only 25 kms, if one LPT is installed in a distt. still the entire distt. is not covered, leaving out number of villages and towns. To cover entire country, more LPTs are needed, linked either by satellite or microwave.

Even in developed countries, the programmes of Television are mostly limited to certain area and there cannot by any External Service due to the limited radiation power of the transmitter. To listen programmes of the countries, we have to use Radio. TV becomes useless. And this is the reason, why radio survived in developed countries even after fast expansion of TV network.

"I said that the sixties were the decade of TV. of course TV cought on like a house on fire, but radio by no means disappeared from the scene." says Narayan Menon, "in 1960 and 70, Western Europe had about 82 million radio sets. By 1970 it had doubled to over 164 million. Japan's 20 million sets more than quadrupled to 87 millions sets in 10 years, the USA's 156 million sets increased to 320 million (imagine 320 million sets for about 215 million people) and Canada's 9 million grew into 21 million in the same period."[8]

This shows that the progress of radio did not stop due to the expansion of TV even in the developed world, where programmes on TV are available on five to six channels from 6 a.m. or say 7 a.m. in the morning till past midnight, continuously. And hence Radio is still an effective medium of communication in the world.

Total Hours of Broadcast / Telecast

Total programme composition of AIR in 1982 was some 5,72,329 hours as against 46,000 hours of TV. And so far the broadcast of classical music is concerned, the yearly total comes to more than 60,000 hours from radio, i.e. some 164 hours per day, through its 102 stations, while total telecast of classical music from TV is not more than half an hour per day for limited amount of audience.[9]

Number of Channels

There are four or five channels of radio in the metropolitan cities, while capital headquarters have atleast two. On the other hand, there is only one channel available for TV programmes, except in the metropolitan cities where second channel has been introduced recently. Regional telecast in so many states has yet to be started which is expected to be completed during Eighth Plan, while Regional Broadcasts from radio were started between 1950.[10]

Production Cost

The greatest limitation of TV programmes is the Production cost. 'TV is an expensive medium.' wrote Narayan Menon. 'An hour of TV programming cost several times as much as an hour of sound programming. Studios have to be much larger, equipment and technical facilities more elaborate. Transmitters cost more; cables cost a fortune.'[11]

For broadcast from Radio, you need a microphone and a transmitter, in addition to one studio and you can cover the whole world. Hence, communication through radio is more suited in India as technically the process of broadcasting from studio or outside locations for reception virtually anywhere within the range of the transmitter has become more efficient and less costly.

Expansion of TV network is based on hardware component. Number of relay transmitters are going on increasing without caring about the suitable programme production. 'Is Doordarshan equipped with software?' asks Shri Mathur, 'Apparently not much has been learnt by the experience of SITE in this area. No suitable staff has been identified, recruited and trained to plan and devise suitable formats and presentation of programmes to match intellectual, cultural and social aspirations and expectations of the people living in those area.'[12]

The programmes of TV are produced for urban elite and not much attention is paid for area specific rural programmes. 'Most of the programmes are half-hearted attempts to provide urban entertainment for the actual viewer. The costly television sets are owned by the well-to-do and so the programmes tend to cater them.'[13] says Ms. Vimala Shastry.

Cheaper to Common Man

Compare the cost of the Television set with radio set taking in view the poverty line in India. One can get a radio set in 50 rupees while minimum cost of a television set is around 3000/-. 'Radio is far cheaper and the availability of cheap transistors has made it ubiquitous.'[14] says N.L. Chawla, an eminent broadcaster.

Mobility / Portability

Apart from the other advantages like cost, number of channels, variety of programmes, mobility and portability are other advantageous factors of radio owners. "With radio, the rest of your life does not stop." says C.R. Ramaswami, "Just as someone may talk to you while you make an omelette, make a bed or washup, your transistor talks to you. It is this freedom that radio bestows on its listeners that sets it apart from television and makes it potent."[15]

On the other hand, it is portable. You can carry it on bicycle, bullock cart, riksha or even in your pocket. Farmers can enjoy music while working in fields. For urban elite, car radios are the best way of communication, one can listen while driving. "In recent years a wider audience has become available through the rapid growth in the number of car radios, and the development of cheap pocket transistors. The remarkable situation has now been reached where by there are more radios sets in Britain than there are people."[16]

Similarly in 'United States, it is estimated that there are some 100 million sets in automobiles alone. . . In Canada, in the UK, in Europe, in Japan, you can hardly get into a car or a taxi without a radio. And of course in developing countries, broadcasting really means sound radio. Television has not yet made any major impact.'[17]

The quality of mobility and portability, more than any other single factor has helped radio to survive as mass medium in the face of competition, from television. This factor is more important in the case of listening of classical music where sound is the only way of communciation.

BEST MEDIUM FOR MUSIC

Taking in view the above factors, it has now become clear that there is no competition of radio from TV, particularly in India. There is, however, another factor which asserts the importance of radio, "All that a radio needs on the other hand is a pair of ears." says C.R. Ramaswamy. "While television requires eye-sight as well as hearing and the ability to read too."[18]

There must be place for television to stand and space to view it, what more total concentration to the exclusion of all else. "Radio is the oldest of the broadcast media, and the simplest. The ear is the main source for information and, as a carrier of the spoken word and music, sound radio is direct and un-complicated."[19]

And view of P.C. Chatterjee are also similar. "Next to news the programmes which command the highest listening are of course *music*. Music is par excellence, the stuff of radio, and it is given very little time on Doordarshan. High and low brow, devotional music, the gazal, modern lyrics, film music and pop, all have their fans, and it is here that AIR could score over the screen."[20] Moreover, it has also had a marked impact on the nature of programming as listening to the radio has become more and more accompaniment to some other activity.

Hence, finally, the fact remains, that Television is not a rival or threate to radio so far as the listening of classical music is concerned.

References

1. Narayan Menon, *The Communication Revolution,* p. 41.
2. H.R. Luthra, *Indian Broadcasting*, pp. 407 and 408.
3. *Ibid.*
4. K.S. Duggal, *Indian Broadcast Media Year Book-1982*, p. 43.
5. H.R. Luthra, *Indian Broadcasting*, p. 408.
6. P.C. Chatterjee in an Article 'AIR Still Has Edge on TV-1', published in *Daily Hindustan Times* of 3rd March, 1988, and table 10.
7. *Ibid.*
8. Narayan Menon, *The Communication Revolution*, p. 41.
9. From Table 12 (Appendix).
10. *Ibid.*
11. Narayan Menon, *The Communication Revolution*, p. 42.
12. R.P. Mathur, in Souvenir of PSA Convention-1982, in an article.
13. Km. Vimala Shastry in an article published in PSA Souvenir-1978.
14. N.L. Chawla, in an article, Published in Souvenir-1978-PSA.
15. C.R. Ramaswami in PSA Souvenir-1980.
16. Lord Windlesham, *Broadcasting in Free Society*, p. 103.
17. Narayan Menon, *The Communication Revolution*, p. 41.
18. C.R. Ramaswamy in an article, Souvenir PSA, AIR, 1980.
19. Lord Windlesham in *Broadcasting in Free Society*, p. 103.
20. P.C. Chatterjee, in an article- 'AIR Has Edge on TV-II', in *Daily Hindustan Times*, 4th March, 1988.

13

Concluding

Radio has an edge over all other mode of communications which is now a well established fact. There is no dispute or doubt that its resonating echoes can change the psyche and taste of society in a shortest period of time, particularly in the case of music, where it reached masses.

"The power of radio to involve people in depth is manifested in its use during homework by youngsters and by many many other people who carry transistor sets in order to provide a private world for themselves amidst crowds. There is a little poem by the German dramatist, Berthold Brecht:

You little box, held to me
when escaping,
So that your valves should
not break,
Carried from house to ship
from ship to train,
So that my enemies might
go on talking to me,
Near my bed, to my pain
The last thing at night, the
First thing in the morning,
of their victories and of my cares,

Promise me not to go silent
all of a sudden."[1]

There are more and more demands to increase the duration of different programmes by variety of listeners and demand of film music is ever increasing. But it is the responsibility of the institution to exploit the potential of the media which has got the power of change the attitudes of the developing society.

Development does not necessarily mean economic development. There should be social development, cultural development, and development in the taste, way of thinking, ideology, etc. There is no question of saving classical music from extinction. The traditions are all established and there is no fear of it dying out. In the last twenty years, the percentage of music programmes has decreased considerably, while number of broadcasting stations has goneup. It one programme is imposed at the cost of other, it will be an act to pleasing one group by ignoring other.

There is an argument in general that no body listens to the classical music and broadcast of such programmes is wastage of time. It is most unfortunate, that this argument, sometimes, given by well educated persons who favour reduction in classical music hours. This is the most undesirable argument given by those who do not understand the origin and richness of our ancient tradition. It has been proved, that listening of classical music is more in South where the literacy is highest. The understanding will definitely improve with the increase in literacy figures.

There are different arguments by the different groups and experts. Politicians want more coverage of development activities. Educationists are interested in educational broadcasts, while some give importance to the rural programmes. Most of the listeners and masses in general are interested in light and film music, while musicians and musicologists are asking for more classical music programmes.

Then what should be really done? The answer is not so easy. "It is impossible for any individual, without access to all the relevant information, to suggest the blue-print of the organisation of broadcasting, and to work out its financial and administrative implications. Nor can such an important and complex matter be left to the limited experience and knowledge of any one person....these and other fundamental questions can only be decided by those, competent to do so."[2]

There are number of arguments in defining the policy and norms of broadcasting. Following the patterns of developed world, where most of the audience is well aware and organised, purpose will not be served. "In the developing societies, the role of broadcasting is far more compreshensive. It has to be used as an instrument for the social and economic development and on the other hand it has to function as a *patron of culture.*"

Out of three objectives of a broadcasting institution viz; Information, Education and Entertainment, the music programmes are generally taken as a part of entertainment, hence not much importance is given to the production and innovation. For music programmes, same old patterns of 1952 are being followed, till now.

The need of the hour is to reorganise the structure of programme planning as the classical and light classical music programmes are not only the programmes for entertainment but are also for education and better communication.

Should'nt we know something about our pioneers and patrons of culture? During Mughal period the education of music was compulsory as a part of training to the Princes in addition to politics, history, fighting, etc. Even Aurangzeb was a great musician. Other Mughal Emperer, kings and rulers were great patrons of music.

The goal of national integration can be achieved by increasing the scope of our music traditions and creating interest of our people in the ideals of Indian traditions of learning. There are Hindus, Brahmins, Christians, Parsis, and Muslims, all are involved with the same enthusiastic approach. Most of the muslim musicians are the disciple of Hindu Gurus and Pandits, there are Muslim Ustads to whom most of the Hindu disciples are attracted. Their traditions are based on the culture and not on religion. In addition to the music programmes, such traditions may be highlighted in music lesson and music lecture programmes.

In 1952, when the slogan 'Popularising Classical Music' was sought, number of stations started music lesson programmes. But in the course of time, this trend has died. The usefulness of the music lesson programmes can be assessed by the popularity gained by 'Sangeet Sarita' programme broadcast from Vividh Bharati. Such short duration programmes can be more useful and may be frequently broadcast from Regional and other stations.

Another successful way in this regard is to introduce 'request programmes' of classical music, from AIR stations, as AIR has done in the case of film and folk music. At present Vividh Bharati is doing well and a weekly request programme of classical music is broadcasting at 3-15 p.m.

The technique of broadcasting is another factor, which depends on the creative skill of programmers. There are number of old broadcasters who introduced certain norms and traditions for successful broadcasting. They generally asked one question 'who is the successful broadcaster?' and replied themselves, 'whose programmes, a listener continue to listen. If a listener switches off his radio set, or turn-over to other station, the integrity of the broadcaster is doubtful.' A successful broadcaster has a quality of making attractive programmes even on dull themes.

Plannning of music programmes is rather more difficult than other programmes. Particularly in the case of classical music, where so many factors are involved. Selection of Raga, suitable time, ratio of vocal and instrumental music, representation of different shades are few factors to be considered. The other goal in this field is to 'Generate Listeners' and to motivate them. The presentation of programme also plays important role in making the programme worth listening. Earlier, great care was taken while broadcasting classical music programmes and the Music Producer was consulted by the announcers for correct details. Even the filler played (in case the programme fell short) was suitably selected. A presenter can play an important role in winning or loosing the listeners.

Since, AIR is maintaining its high standards and graded artists are invited by AIR and TV, there is no scope for encouragement to the new and emerging artists in general programmes. Due to the delays in audition results, an artist, who is not approved by the audition board is very much discouraged and does not dare to appear again for the audition. Something will have to be done in the case of such artists.

Past and future development of the broadcasting in India is mainly based on the installation of new transmitters, in order to cover more area and population. This is the best and quickest way to achieve physical targets. But in fact it has never been understood, what programmes are broadcast from these transmitters? "It was either forgotten or not understood that in the absence of adequate facilities to the programmers, the huge expenditure on the installation and maintenance of such transmitters would be unjustified.

Due to the development of the hardware component, the balance between the Engineering and Programme staff has been shattered considerably, which resulted less promotion opportunities to programme people. This is creating frustration among programme staff and ultimately affecting the quality of broadcast. A radio station is a cultural organisation and not an office of the Electricity Board. Its basic purpose is programme."[3]

The need of the hour is to establish full fledge Research and Development wing for programmes to create new variety in the modality and methodology of programme planning, production and development, so that the broadcasts are research *oriented.* Lot have been done and still much have to be done in this field.

Creativity and credibility are the main objectives of broadcasting which can be achieved by involvement of the individuals with professional competence. The broadcasting is a profession and should be managed by the professionals, experts and broadcasters.

The success of a broadcasting organisation does not necessarily depends in achieving physical targets, like population and area covered, such developments are reducing a cultural organisation to an industry to manufacture programmes. AIR and TV are the patrons of art, culture and literature where quality counts first, and not data oriented development. And only Research oriented broadcast can achieve the targets in the fast changing world.

References

1. Marshall Mcluhan, *Understanding Media*, p. 298.
2. Mehra Masani, *Broadcasting and the People.*
3. M.S. Bedi, President DSA, in Presidential speech.

Appendix

TABLE 1

Growth of AIR Network Since Independence

Period	*No. of Sta-tions*	*No. of Transmitter MW/SW/FM*	*Coverage from population percentage*	*M.W. Area*
15-8-1947	6*	18	11	2.5
1-14-1951	26	46	20	12.0
31-3-1956 End of 1st Five Year Plan	28	46	46	31.00
31-3-1961 End of 2nd Plan	34	59	55	37
31-3-1966 End of 3rd Plan	56	110	70	52
31-3-1969	69	127	73	56
31-3-1974	75	140	80.3	67.5
31-3-1980	86	157	89.40	77.75
31-3-1987	92	172	95	86
18-10-1990	102	180	96	86 Appr.
31-1-1993	148	244	96.20	86.10

* Five more broadcasting stations were taken over subsequently from the princely states: Hyderabad, Aurangabad, Mysore, Trivendrum and Baroda.

Number of stations include auxiliary centres which later converted to fulfledged stations.

Sources:

(i) *Indian Broadcasting-Media-Year book* by K.S. Duggal, pp. 5 and 6.

(ii) H.R. Luthra's, *Indian Broadcasting*.

(iii) Shri S.K. Sharma's Lecture on 8-10-90 at STI- and two stations Murshidabad and Alwar included later (Local stations).

(vi) *Mass Media in India 1993*-Publication Division.

TABLE 2

Programme Composition

	PROGRAMME	*DURATION*		*PER-CENTAGE*
1960				
	Music	50,981		47.06
	Shoban word & News	57,275		52.94
	TOTAL	1,08,256		100.00
	VIVIDH BHARATI	7,123		
	G. TOTAL	**1,15,379**	Hrs.	
1961				
	Music	51,184		46.7
	Shoban word and News	58,150		53.3
	TOTAL	1,09,334		100.0
	VIVIDH BHARATI	7,931		
	G. TOTAL	**1,17,265**		
1975				
	Music	1,21,285		40.8
	Shoban word and News	1,76,196		59.2
	TOTAL	2,97,481		100.0
	VIVIDH BHARATI	1,41,198		
	G. TOTAL	**4,38,680**		
1980				
	Music	1,58,829		40.60
	Shoban word & News	2,32,417		59.40
	TOTAL	**3,91,246**		100.00

Sources:

1. *Broadcasting in India*, G.C. Awasthy (For 60-61)
2. *Mass Media in India*, I&B Ministry, 1978.
3. *Indian Broadcasting Media*, K.S. Duggal, 1982.

TABLE 3

Composition and Duration of Home Service Programme 1975

	Type of Prog.	*Duration*		*Per-centage*
		Hrs.	*Mts.*	
1.	Classical Vocal	24,721	02	8.3
2.	Classical Instrumental	22,376	18	7.5
3.	Folk Music (Vocal)	9,354	14	3.1
4.	Folk Instrumental	99	3	0.1
5.	Light Vocal	25,768	46	8.7
6.	Light Instrumental	3,485	56	1.2
7.	Devotional Music	13,862	2	4.7
8.	Film Music	16,176	23	5.4
9.	Western Music	5,444	32	1.8
10.	Talks discussion	28,070	57	9.4
11.	Drama-Feature	11,605	42	3.9
12.	News	69,245	1	23.3
13.	Religions	382	52	0.3
14.	Children	3,695	52	1.2
15.	Women	4,142	29	1.3
16.	Rural	18,096	30	6.1
17.	Industrial	4,257	36	1.4
18.	Armed Forces	4,352	47	1.5
19.	Tribal	4,531	48	1.5
20.	Educational	7,077	49	2.3
21.	Publicity	5,979	26	2.0
22.	Others	14,754	41	5.0
	TOTAL	2,97,481	46	100.00
	Vividh Bharati	1,14,198	14	–
	G. TOTAL	4,38,680	–	–

Source: Mass Media in India, Publication Division, I&B Ministry, 1978, p. 23.

TABLE 4

Programme Composition during 1980

	Classifications	*Durations*		*Per-centage*
		Hrs.	*Mts.*	
1.	Classical Music	47,407	00	12.12
2.	Folk Music	15,399	22	3.94
3.	Light Music	32,465	52	8.29
4.	Devotional Music	19,819	40	5.07
5.	Western Music	16,981	56	4.34
6.	Film Music	26,758	02	6.84
7.	Spoken Word	35,168	48	8.99
8.	Drama Feature	13,270	10	3.99
9.	News	90,609	44	23.16
10.	Religion	355	00	0.14
11.	Children	4,216	16	1.08
12.	Women	5,477	00	1.40
13.	Rural	20,969	12	5.36
14.	Industrial	8,030	04	2.05
15.	Youth	11,164	48	2.85
16.	Armed Forces	4,721	22	1.20
17.	Tribal	9,577	16	2.45
18.	Others	7,804	44	1.99
19.	Educational	12,473	12	3.19
20.	Publicity	8,405	30	2.15
	TOTAL	3,91,246	00	100.00

Source: Indian Broadcasting Media Year-Book 1982, K.S. Duggal, p. 38.

TABLE 5

Composition of Programmes (Home Service)

Type of Prog.	*Hrs.*	*Mts.*	*Percentage*
Music	1,55,869	57	36.11
News	95,697	30	22.17
Spoken word	1,80,085	52	41.72
TOTAL	4,31,653	19	100.00
Vividh Bharati	1,40,675	56	
G. TOTAL	5,72,329	15	

Composition of Music Programme

Music	*Hrs.*	*Mts.*	*Percentage*
Classical	52,143	42	33.46
Folk	16,100	41	10.34
Light	33,625	46	21.57
Devotional	21,927	58	14.06
Film	27,150	58	17.42
Western	4,920	52	3.15
TOTAL	1,55,869	57	100.00

Source: Mass Media in India 1981-83 Ministry of I & B, p. 137.

TABLE 6

Music Programmes

Year	*B'east Hrs. Total*	*Devoted to Music Hrs.*	*Percentage*
1937-38			74.00
1960	1,08,256	50,981	47.06
1961	1,17,265	51,184	46.70
1975	2,97,481	1,21,285	40.80
1980	3,91,246	1,58,831	40.60
1982	4,31,653	1,55,869	36.11
VIVIDH BHARATI			+
1960		7,123	
1961		7,931	
1975		1,41,198	
1982		1,40,675	

Sources:

1. *Broadcasting in India*, G.C. Awasthy, p. 33.
2. *Mass Media in India,* 1978, I&B Ministry, p. 23.
3. *Indian Broadcasting Media*, Year Book 1982, K.S. Duggal, p. 3.
4. *Mass Media in India*, 1981-83, I&B Ministry, p. 137.

TABLE 7

Programme Composition Home Service [Percentage] (1983)

Categories	*Percentage*
Classical Music	12.8
Folk Music	3.6
Light Music	11.3
Film Music	6.1
Wester Music	4.3
News and Current Affairs	24.6
Talk Discussions	6.8
Sports	4.8
Drama Feature	3.7
Rural	6.3
Educational	3.7
Children	1.1
Women	1.6
Industrial	1.2
Armed Forces	1.6
Tribal	1.9
Publicity and Others	4.6

Source: Broadcasting in India, P.C. Chatterjee, p. 138.

TABLE 8

Vividh Bharati Total Hours of Broadcast

Year	*In a Weak*	*Yearly Hrs.*
3rd October 1957	Week days 5 Hrs. Sunday & Holidays - 7½ Hrs.	1,995
2nd October 1963	Week days 11¼ Hrs. Sundays & Holidays 11¾ Hrs.	4,140
1973	Week days 12-10 Hrs. Sundays & Holidays 12-40 Hrs.	1,41,198
1982	—do—	1,40,675

Sources: 1. *Broadcasting in India*, G.C. Awasthi.
2. *Mass Media in India*, 1978 & 1983. I&B Ministry.

TABLE 9

National and other Important Programmes

	Programme	*Started From*
1.	National Programme Music (Weekly)	20-7-1952
2.	Talk English (Weekly)	29-4-1953
3.	Talk Hindi Weekly	August 1963
4.	Discussion English	29-4-1953
5.	Discussion Hindi	August 1962
6.	Plays - Monthly	26-7-1956
7.	Features - Monthly	15-3-1956
8.	Party Political Broadcasts	June 1977
9.	Radio Sangeet Sammelan	1954
10.	Sardar Patel Memorial Lectures	1955
11.	Dr. Rajendra Prasad Memorial Lectures	1957
12.	Symposium of Posts	1956
13.	Akashwani Annual Awards	1974

Source : *Indian Broadcasting Media Year Book 1982*, K.S. Duggal, p. 39.

TABLE 10

Growth of Listening

Year	*No. of Radio Sets*	
July 1927	1,000	
31-12-1927	3,594	
1928	6,152	
1929	7,775	
1930	7,719	
1932	8,557	
1933	10,872	
1934	16,179	
1935	24,839	
1936	37,797	
1937	50,680	
1938	64,480	
1939	1,00,439	
1940	1,28,379	
1945	2,17,045	
1947	2,75,955	
1948	3,18,990	
1949	4,08,060	
1950	5,46,319	
1951	6,85,508	
1955	10,29,816	
1960	21,42,754	
1962	25,98,608	
1965	54,05,973	
1970	1,18,36,653	
1971	1,27,72,228	
1972	1,28,94,535	
1973	1,40,33,919	
1974	1,48,48,097	
1975	1,67,72,943	
1979	2,06,74,113	
1980		Licence fee
1988	6,00,00,000	withdrawn
1990	9,50,00,000	
1992	12,00,00,000	(Estimated)

Sources:

(i) *Broadcasting in India*, G.C. Awasthy, p. 259 (1927 to 1962)

(ii) *Mass Media in India 1978*, Publication Division, p. 241 (1964 to 1975)

(iii) *Indian Broadcasting Media*, K.S. Duggal, p. 35 (1979)

(iv) *Mass Media in India*, Publication Division, 1981-83, p. 218

(v) *Report of Electronic Commission* quoted by Shri P.C. Chattergee & Sunil Mishra.

TABLE 11

List of Countries with which Cultural Exchange Programme have been signed (1982)

1. Afghanistan
2. Algeria
3. Australia
4. Bulgaria
5. Belgium
6. Brazil
7. Columbia
8. Cuba
9. Cyprus
10. Czechoslovakia
11. Egypt
12. France
13. Germany (DR)
14. Ghana
15. Federal Republic of Germany
16. Hungary
17. Iran
18. Iraq
19. Italy
20. Japan
21. North Korea
22. South Korea
23. Kenya
24. Lessothe
25. Malaysia
26. Mauritius
27. Mexico
28. Mongolia
29. Morocco
30. Mozambique
31. Netherlands
32. Poland
33. Portugal
34. Romania
35. Senegal
36. Sri Lanka
37. Syria
38. Tunisia
39. Turkey
40. Uganda
41. U.S.S.R.
42. Vietnam
43. Yogoslavia
44. Yemen
45. Zambia
46. Zimbabwe

Source: Indian Broadcasting Media, Year Book 1982, K.S. Duggal, p. 60.

TABLE 12

Comperative Study of Radio and TV in India

Particulars	*Radio*	*Television*
1982		
No. of Stations	86	11
No. of Transmitters	162	41
Population covered	89.65 %	19.11 %
Area Covered	78.83 %	6.74 %
No. of Sets	1,22,00,725	21,90,957
Total Prog. Hrs.	5,72,329	46,000
1987		
No. of Stations	92	11
No. of Transmitters	170	225
Population covered	95 %	52 %
1990		
No. of Stations	102	11
No. of transmitters	172	425 approx
Population covered	96 %	72 % approx.
Area covered	87 %	50 % approx.
No. of sets	9,50,00,000	2,00,00,000

Sources:

(a) Radio and TV Chapters of *Indian Broadcasting Media*, Year Book 1982, K.S. Duggal.

(b) *Broadcasting in India*, P.C. Chatterjee, p. 56.

(c) *Daily Hindustan Times* 3-3-1988 from P.C. Chatterjee's article.

(d) Lecture by Shri Sunil Mishra, Director, *Audience Research*, New Delhi on 23-1-1990.

TABLE 13

Comparative Listening Percentage of Sangeet Sarita Programme

	DELHI		*BOMBAY*		*CALCUTTA*		*MADRAS*	
	Weekdays	*Sunday*	*Weekdays*	*Sunday*	*Weekdays*	*Sunday*	*Weekdays*	*Sunday*
Urban								
BASE N	586	586	600	600	600	600	590	598
LIGHT MUSIC (Mini) (NON FILM)	4	4	4	3	1	0	1	4
SANGEET SARITA	18	20	20	20	5	3	6	5
FILM MUSIC (Max)	36	38	39	43	17	16	7	6
Rural								
BASE N	297	296	299	300	299	298	300	288
LIGHT MUSIC (Mini)	2	4	6	13	1	0	1	1
SANGEET SARITA	8	13	25	21	1	1	3	2
FILM MUSIC (Max)	26	30	39	39	22	19	6	7

TABLE 14

Percentage Listening of VB Classical Music Programmes

	DELHI		*BOMBAY*		*CALCUTTA*		*MADRAS*	
	Weekdays	*Sunday*	*Weekdays*	*Sunday*	*Weekdays*	*Sunday*	*Weekdays*	*Sunday*
Urban								
BASE N	586	599	600	600	600	600	590	598
SANGEET SARITA	18	20	20	20	5	3	6	5
SWAR SUDHA	3	0	7	6	2	0	2	1
ANURAGINI	0	–	3	–	1	–	1	–
Rural								
BASE N	297	296	299	300	299	298	300	288
SANGEET SARITA	8	13	25	21	1	1	1	2
SWAR SUDHA	2	5	13	9	0	1	1	2
ANURAGINI	3	–	2	–	0	–	0	–

TABLE 15

Frequency of Listening to VB in a Week

(Figures are in Percentage)

	IN A WEEK	*DELHI*	*BOMBAY*	*CALCUTTA*	*MADRAS*
	BASE-N				
	Urban	1772	1794	1800	1783
1.	6–7 Days	76	70	41	79
2.	3–5 Days	13	18	23	12
3.	1–2 Days	4	6	20	4
4.	LESS OFTEN	4	3	10	2
5.	NEVER	1	1	3	1
	BASE-N				
	Rural	876	899	893	878
1.	6–7 Days	64	83	49	83
2.	3–5 Days	18	9	20	11
3.	1–2 Days	8	5	10	2
4.	LESS OFTEN	4	1	15	1
5.	NEVER	4	0	4	0

TABLE 16

All India Listening

Tunning of Air Stations for Music Programmes

(Percentage of Respondents)

Programme Type	*Area*	*North Zone*	*Central Zone*	*East Zone*	*West Zone*	*South Zone*	*All India*
Film Music	Urban	77.0	80.2	72.3	84.4	92.1	80.9
	Rural	73.0	79.5	74.1	68.3	91.4	78.2
Devotional Music	Urban	27.3	31.7	43.3	50.3	53.6	44.2
	Rural	35.9	38.5	56.0	71.0	52.4	49.2
Light Music	Urban	25.8	40.7	31.4	37.4	45.9	35.8
	Rural	21.9	32.3	39.6	44.8	39.2	34.7
Folk Music	Urban	19.9	23.5	28.1	33.0	27.1	25.7
	Rural	47.6	37.9	40.0	30.6	35.4	39.2
Classical Music	Urban	8.0	10.9	21.5	17.2	34.9	19.8
	Rural	3.6	3.9	9.3	7.4	12.7	7.8

Source: This is All India Radio, U.L. Baruah, p. 251.

TABLE 17

Names of Music Artists of Different Radio Programmes and Radio Sangeet Sammelan

S. No.	Name	Type
1.	Anant Lal & Party	Shehnai
2.	Parveen Sultana	Vocal
3.	Munawwar Ali Khan	Vocal
4.	S. Balachander	Veena
5.	D.K. Datar	Violin
6.	C. Saroja & C. Lalita	Vocal
7.	Rajan Mishra Sajan Mishra	Vocal
8.	Uma Shanker Mishra	Sitar
9.	M.L. Vasanthakumari	Vocal
10.	Malvika Kanan	Vocal
11.	Raghunath Seth	Flute
12.	Ghulam Mustafa Khan	Vocal
13.	Nivrittibua Sarnaik	Vocal
14.	Mehmood Mirza	Sitar
15.	Alathur S. Srinivasa Iyer	Vocal
16.	M.P.N. Sethuraman & M.P.N. Ponnuswami	Nagaswaram
17.	Kumar Gandharva	Vocal
18.	Padmavati Saligram	Vocal
19.	K.V. Narayanaswami	Vocal
20.	Prapancham Sitaram	Flute
21.	Sheik Hussain Saheb	Clrionet
22.	Amjad Ali Khan	Sarod
23.	A. Subba Rao	Vocal
24.	K.S. Narayanaswami	Veena
25.	T.T. Seetha	Vocal
26.	Bismilla Khan & Party	Shehnai
27.	Bhimsen Joshi	Vocal
28.	Shiv Kumar Sharma	Santoor
29.	Nirmala Arun	Vocal
30.	Budhaditya Mukherjee	Sitar
31.	Prabha Atre	Vocal
32.	M.Balamurli Krishna	Violin
33.	Radha & Jayalaxmi	Vocal

(Continued)

S. No.	*Name*	*Type*
34.	Imrat Hussain Khan	Sitar
35.	Sheila Dhar	Vocal
36.	Jaya Biswas	Sitar
37.	R. Pichumani	Veena
38.	Sreerangam Gopalarathnam	Vocal
39.	Hari Prasad Chaurasia	Flute
40.	Kishori Amonker	Vocal
41.	T. Rukmini	Violin
42.	Seerkazhi S. Govindarajan	Vocal
43.	Brij Bhushanlal Kabra	Guitar
44.	Gangubai Hangal	Vocal
45.	Satyadev Pawar	Violin
46.	Tejpal Singh & Surinder Singh	Vocal
47.	Samta Prasad	Tabla
48.	Asad Ali Khan	Been
49.	Hiradevi Mishra	Vocal
50.	Ashok Roy	Sarod
51.	Basavraj Rajguru	Vocal
52.	Rita Ganguli	Vocal
53.	Indranil Bhattacharya	Sitar
54.	AIR Madras Vadya Vrind Unit	—
55.	Madurai S. Somasundaram	Vocal
56.	Laxmi Shanker	Vocal
57.	V.G. Jog	Violin
58.	M.V. Ramamurthy	Vocal
59.	T.M. Tyagarajan	Vocal
60.	Sheik Chinnamoula Saheb	Nagaswaram
61.	Sunil Mukherjee	Sarod
62.	Prabhudeo Sardar	Vocal
63.	T.N. Krishnan	Violin
64.	Maharajapuram Santhanam	Vocal
65.	Debabrata Chaudhury	Sitar
66.	Hafeez Ahmed Khan	Vocal
67.	M.V. Varahswami	Gottruvadiam
68.	V. Ramachandran	Vocal
69.	N.S. Srinivasan	Flute
70.	R.K. Srikantan	Vocal

(Continued)

S. No.	*Name*	*Type*
71.	Chittubabu	Veena
72.	Mani Krishnaswami	Vocal
73.	Rangnayaki Rajgopalan	Veena
74.	D.K. Pattammal	Vocal
75.	Buddhadev Dasgupta	Sarod
76.	Jitendra Abhisheki	Vocal
77.	Mushtaq Ali Khan	Sitar
78.	Lalgudi G. Jayaraman	Violin
79.	Nandlal Ghose	Sarod
80.	Ram Chatur Mallik	Vocal
81.	Madurai T.N. Seshagopalan	Vocal
82.	T.S. Shankaran	Flute
83.	M.S. Subbalaxmi	Vocal
84.	Gopal Krishnan	Vichitra Veena
85.	Nasir Zahiruddin Dagar and Nasir Faiyazuddin Dagar	Vocal
86.	Ali Ahmed Hussain & Party	Shehnai
87.	Prakash Wadera	Flute
88.	Naina Devi	Vocal
89.	Jagannath Pacherwal & Party	Shehnai
90.	Dinkar Kaikani	Vocal
91.	Yemni Shanker Shastri	Veena
92.	Devendra Murdeshwar	Flute
93.	Mani Prasad	Vocal
94.	M.S. Ramanathan	Vocal
95.	A.K.C. Natarajan	Clarionet
96.	Arvind Parekh	Sitar
97.	S.P. Natarajan	Sitar
98.	Voleti Venkateshwarulu	Vocal
99.	M. Chandrashekharan	Violin
100.	Jayalaxmi Santhanam	Vocal
101.	Jagdish Prasad Pandit	Vocal
102.	Shobha Gurtu	Vocal
103.	Manilal Nag	Sitar
104.	Vijay Raghav Rao	Flute
105.	Sharafat Hussain Khan	Vocal

(Continued)

S. No.	*Name*	*Type*
106.	Sikkil V. Kunjumani & N.Leela	Vocal
107.	Bahadur Khan	Sarod
108.	L.K. Pandit	Vocal
109.	S.R.D. Muthukumarswami & S.R.D. Vaidyanathan	Nagaswaram
110.	Sabri Khan	Sarangi
111.	Nasir Aminuddin Dagar	Vocal
112.	N. Rajam	Violin
113.	Binapani Mishra	Vocal
114.	Kishan Maharaj	Tabla
115.	Sisirkona Dhar Chauthuri	Violin
116.	Niaz Ahmed and Faiaz Ahmed	Vocal
117.	Srikant Bakre	Vocal
118.	Kalyani Roy	Sitar
119.	Sulochna Brahaspati	Vocal
120.	C. Krishnamurthy	Veena
121.	Nadunuri Krishnamurthy	Vocal
122.	Sharan Rani	Sarod
123.	N. Ramani	Flute
124.	R. Vedavalli	Vocal
125.	Malti Pande	Vocal
126.	T.R. Subramaniam	Vocal
127.	Tanjavur K.P. Sivanandam & Sarda Sivanandam	Veena
128.	Puducode K. Krishnamurthy	Vocal
129.	Abdul Halim Jafar Khan	Sitar
130.	Zarin Daroowala	Sarod
131.	Pandit Mani Ram	Vocal
132.	B.N. Suresh	Flute
133.	Mallikarjun Mansoor	Vocal
134.	Coddalore M. Subramaniam	Vocal
135.	Pandit Ramnarain	Sarangi
136.	B.V. Raman and B.V. Lakshamanan	Vocal
137.	Sarafat Hussain Khan	Vocal
138.	Bimal Mukherjee	Sitar
139.	Siaram Tivari	Vocal
140.	Chhatrapati Singh	Pakhawaj

(Continued)

S. No.	*Name*	*Type*
141.	M.S. Balasubramaniya Sarma	Vocal
142.	Domada Chitti Abbayi	Nagaswaram
143.	Ramesh Prem	Vichitra Veena
144.	V.L. Jankiram	Veena
145.	Dayashanker & Party	Shehnai
146.	Rasiklal Andharia	Vocal

Source : This is All India Radio, U.L. Baruah, p. 309.

TABLE 18

Recordings of Old Masters in AIR Archives

S. No.	*Name of the artist*	*Duration*
1.	Abdul Karim Khan	20 mts.
2.	Abdul Wahid Khan	120 mts.
3.	Abid Hussain	180 mts.
4.	Alathur Brothers	620 mts.
5.	Allauddin Khan	240 mts.
6.	Ali Akbar Khan	720 mts.
7.	Ajodhya Prasad	120 mts.
8.	Amir Khan	1020 mts.
9.	Arunachalam Kurukurchi	280 mts.
10.	Asad Ali Khan	60 mts.
11.	Bade Gulam Ali Khan	840 mts.
12.	Badi Moti Bai	80 mts.
13.	Beharebua G.R.	300 mts.
14.	Balasubramaniam G.N.	180 mts.
15.	Barodekar Hirabai	640 mts.
16.	Begum Akhtar	2460 mts.
17.	Bhagawathar Kalyanakrishna	60 mts.
18.	Bhole Jyotsna	100 mts.
19.	Bismillah Khan and Party	1500 mts.
20.	Brinda and Mukta	380 mts.
21.	Bundu Khan	160 mts.
22.	Chembai Vaidyanatha Bhagawathar	80 mts.
23.	Chand Khan	100 mts.
24.	Chaubey Laxman Prasad	20 mts.
25.	Chaudhuri Virendrakishore Roy	40 mts.
26.	Chowdiah T.	240 mts.
27.	Dabir Khan Mohd	40 mts.
28.	Dagar Brothers-Nasir Zahiruddin Dagar & Nasir Faiyazuddin Dagar	600 mts.
29.	Desigar M.M. Dandapani	80 mts.
30.	Faiyaz Khan	1700 mts.
31.	Farhat Jahan Biboo	20 mts.
32.	Kumar Gandharva	200 mts.
33.	Ghose Pannalal	720 mts.

(Continued)

S. No.	Name of the artist	Duration
34.	Girija Devi	140 mts.
35.	Hafeez Ali Khan	300 mts.
36.	Hirji Bai Doctor	60 mts.
37.	Hangal Gangoobai	340 mts.
38.	Hussanlal Pandit	40 mts.
39.	Iyengar Ariyakudi Ramanuja	760 mts.
40.	Iyengar Dori Swami	160 mts.
41.	Iyer Karaikudi Sambasiva	400 mts.
42.	Iyer Madurai Mani	620 mts.
43.	Iyer Musiri Subramania	100 mts.
44.	Iyer Semangudi Srinivasa	500 mts.
45.	Iyer T.K. Jairama	1660 mts.
46.	Jaddan Bai	20 mts.
47.	Joshi Bhimsen	560 mts.
48.	Joshi Datto Pant K	60 mts.
49.	Joshi Gajanan Rao	1240 mts.
50.	Kabra Damodar	160 mts.
51.	Kanthy Maharaj	60 mts.
52.	Kerkar Kesharbai	20 mts.
53.	Khadim Hussain Khan & Latafat Hussain Khan	40 mts.
54.	Krishnan Ramanand	80 mts.
55.	Lahiri Chimoy	40 mts.
56.	Mahalingam T.R.	100 mts.
57.	Malik Ram Chatur	80 mts.
58.	Mansoor Malikarjun	1740 mts.
59.	Mathur Saran Rani	380 mts.
60.	Maulasaheb Sheikh Chinna	60 mts.
61.	Mishra Gopal	120 mts.
62.	Moitra Radhika Mohan	440 mts.
63.	Mushtaq Hussain Khan	760 mts.
64.	Naidu Dwaram Venkataswami	340 mts.
65.	Narayana Swami K.S.	440 mts.
66.	Nisar Hussain Khan	1100 mts.
67.	Omkar Nath Thakur	920 mts.
68.	Palghat Rama Bhagasathar	80 mts.
69.	Paluskar D.V.	1420 mts.

(Continued)

S. No.	Name of the artist	Duration
70.	Pandit Krishna Shanker Rao	300 mts.
71.	Pantulu Parupalli Ramakrishnayya	180 mts.
72.	Parvartikar D.R.	120 mts.
73.	Pattamal D.K.	660 mts.
74.	Patwardhan Vinayak Rao	760 mts.
75.	Pillai Subramania Palani	40 mts.
76.	Pillai P.S. Veeruswami	200 mts.
77.	Poonchwale Bala Saheb	140 mts.
78.	Rajab Ali Khan	220 mts.
79.	Rajan S. Mayuram	60 mts.
80.	Rajamanikam Kumbakonam	40 mts.
81.	Ramanathan M.D.	120 mts.
82.	Ram Narayan	100 mts.
83.	Rane Saraswati	40 mts.
84.	Rasoolan Bai	380 mts.
85.	Ratanjankar S.N.	740 mts.
86.	Ravi Shanker	380 mts.
87.	Raza Hussain Khan	60 mts.
88.	Shakoor Khan	80 mts.
89.	Sarafat Hussain Khan	540 mts.
90.	Sastri Budalur Krishna Murthy	80 mts.
91.	Sathur A.G. Subramanaiam	80 mts.
92.	Siddeshwari Devi	1000 mts.
93.	Subbalaxmi M.S.	1500 mts.
94.	Sukla Shiv Kumar	60 mts.
95.	Thirakwa Ahmedjan	180 mts.
96.	Vasantha Kumari M.L.	400 mts.
97.	Venkataramaiah K.S.	260 mts.
98.	Vilayat Hussain Khan	2360 mts.
99.	Vyas Narayan Rao	160 mts.
100.	Waze Ramakrishna Bua	40 mts.
101.	Yusuf Ali Khan	300 mts.

Source: U.L. Baruah, *This is All India Radio*, p. 349.

TABLE 19

Statement showing Students of Music influenced by Radio Programmes of Classical Music

Total Number of Students interviewed (Music College and School)		48
Listen to classical music progs. broadcast from radio		
	Regularly	17
	Frequently	11
	Occasionally	16
	Never	4
Listen to Sangeet	Regularly	35
Sarita Prog.	Frequently	3
	Occasionally	8
	Never	2
Influenced by Sangeet Sarita* or other Music Prog.		43

* Students were also influenced by other means like Parents, concerts and relatives etc.

Bibliography

(Primary and Secondary)

A. Books / Publications

Asa Briggs, *The Birth of Broadcasting*, Oxford University Press, London, 1961.

Acharya Brahaspati, *Musalman aur Bhartiya Sangeet* (Hindi), Rajkamal Prakashan Pvt. Ltd., New Delhi.

Acharya Brahaspati, *Sangeet Chintamani* (Hindi), Rajkamal Prakashan Pvt. Ltd., New Delhi.

Anna Sproule, *The Role of Media*, Macdonald, 1986.

A.K. Banerjee, *Hindustani Sangeet:Changing Phases*, Sharda Publishing House, Delhi, 1992.

B.C. Deva, *Musical Instruments*, National Book Trust India, New Delhi.

B.N. Ahuja, *Mass Communication*, Varma Brothers, New Delhi, 1978.

G.C. Awasthy, *Broadcasting in India*, Allied Publishers Pvt. Ltd., Delhi, 1965.

Gowri Kuppuswami & M.Hariharan, *Royal Patronage to Indian Music*

H.R. Luthra, *Indian Broadcasting*, Publication Division, Ministry of I&B, Govt. of India, 1985, New Delhi.

I & B Ministry, *Mass Media in India-1978*, Publication Division, I&B Ministry, Govt. of India, 1979.

I & B Ministry, *Mass Media in India 1981-83*, Publication Division, I&B Ministry, Govt. of India, 1984.

I & B Ministry, *Mass Media in India-1984*, Publication Division, 1985

James Curron & Jean Seaton, *Power without Responsibility-The Press and Broadcasting in Britain.*, Methuen, London, 1985.

J.C.W. Reith, *In To The Wind*, Hodder & Stougton Ltd., London.

Kevel J. Kumar, *Mass Communication in India*, Jaico Publishing House, Delhi, 1981.

Keith Geddes, *Broadcasting in Britain-1922-1972*, Her Majesty's Stationery Office, London, 1972.

K.S. Duggal, *Indian Broadcast Media Year Book-1982*, Marwah Publication, 1983, New Delhi.

Andre Doutsch Ltd., Lord Windlesham, *Broadcasting in Free Society*, Basil Blackwell, Oxford, 1980.

Leonel Fielden, *The Natural Bent*, London, W-1.

Laxmi Narayan Garg, *Hamare Sangeet Ratna* (Hindi), Sangeet Karyalaya, Hathras, 1984.

Marshal Mcluhan, *Understanding Media,* Fifth Impression in 1975 by Routledge and Kegan Paul Ltd., London.

M.R. Gautam, *The Musical Heritage of India.*

Mehra Masani, *Broadcasting and the People,* National Book Trust India, New Delhi, 1976.

Narayan Menon, *The Communication Revolution,* National Book Trust, New Delhi, 1976.

Narayan Menon, *Sanchar Kranti (Hindi)*, National Book Trust, New Delhi, 1976.

P.C. Chatterjee, *Broadcasting in India*, Sage Publications India Pvt. Ltd., New Delhi, 1987.

P.C. Chatterjee, *Two Voices*, Hem Publishers Pvt. Ltd., New Delhi, 1987.

Peggy Holroyde, *Indian Music-A Vast Ocean of Promise*, George Allen and Unwin Ltd., London.

Pt. Ravi Shanker, *My Music My Life*, Vishal Publishing House Pvt. Ltd., New Delhi.

S.K.A. Durga, *Voice Culture.*

S.C. Sharma, *Media Communication and Development,* Rawat Publication, Jaipur, 1987.

Shyam Parmar, *Folk Music and Mass Media,* Communication Publication, New Delhi, 1977.

Sulochna Brahaspati, *Khusrau, Tansen Tatha Anya Kalakar*, Rajkamal Prakashan Pvt. Ltd., New Delhi.

S.P. Jain, *Art of Broadcasting*, Intellectual Publishing House, New Delhi.

Swami Pragyananand, *Historical Development of Indian Music.*

U.L. Baruah, *This is All India Radio*, Publication Division, Ministry of I&B, New Delhi, 1983.

Vasant, *Sangeet Visharad* (Hindi), Sangeet Karyalaya, Hathras.

Pt.V.N. Bhatkhande, *A Short Historical Survey of Music of Upper India.*, Speech Before All India Music Conf. at Baroda, 1916.

B-Survey Reports

Listenership-CBS Audience Research Unit AIR-1980-81.

Listening Report Audience Research Unit AIR-1983, Jullundhur.

Listening Report Audience Research Unit AIR-1984, Calcutta.

C-Magzines and News Papers

Akashvani, 24-30 July, 1977, Spl. Publication on 42nd year of Publication.

A Hand Book for Junior Programme Officers, 1976, DAVP.

Dinman, Hindi Weekly, 16-22 Sept. 1984.

Daily M.P. Chronicle, 19-3-1988, Bhopal Edition.

Daily Hindustan Times, 3rd and 4th March,1988, Published from Delhi.

Daily Alok (Hindi), 21-8-88, Bhopal.

Souvenir, National Convention-Programme Staff Association-AIR New Delhi, 1978.

Souvenir, National Convention-Programme Staff Association-AIR, New Delhi, 1979.

Souvenir, National Convention Programme Staff Association-AIR, New Delhi, 1980.

Souvenir, National Convention Programme Staff Association-AIR, New Delhi, 1982.

Schedule of National Programme Service, Jan-March, 1990. New Delhi.

D-Letters From:

Bala Thomos, Wellington-Access Radio New Zealand, 2-11-1988.

Deeranjan Malve, B.B.C. London, 19-1-1989.

Douglas Ward, Director of Programming, Canadian Broadcasting Corporation, Ottawa, 7-12-1990.

Marir Sorbrati, Radio Sargam & Radio Jagte Raho-Amsterdam, Nederland, 27-1-1989.

Roselyme Cossette, Research Officer, International Relations, CBC, Ottawa, 20-3-1989.

Sudhakaran, Sri Lanka, Colombo, 14-10-1988.

Dr. Sunil Mishra, Director, Audience Research, AIR, PTI Building, New Delhi, 22-9-1988.

Note: Letters written to 52 countries, 20 responded and 7 mentioned above were useful in Chapter-5(iii). Other information collected through interviews.

E-Interviews/Lectures/Other references

Artists

Amjad Ali Khan, Sarod, New Delhi, August-Sept. 1988.

Abdul Latif Khan, Sarangi, AIR, Bhopal, August-Sept. 1988.

Ismail Daddoo Khan, Tabla, AIR, Bhopal, August-Sept. 1988.

Nazar Hussain, Sarangi Player, AIR, Bhopal, August-Sept. 1988.

Rehmat Ali Khan, Sarod Player, AIR, Bhopal, August-Sept. 1988.

S.S. Korwar, Vocal, AIR, Bhopal, August-Sept. 1988.

Experts/Broadcasters

Douglas Ward, Director of Programming, Canadian Broadcasting Corporation, Ottawa, 7-10-1990.

Francis Lucas, Local Radio, Philipines, 7-10-1990.

P.V. Krishnamurthy, Ex-DG, TV & Media Consultant, UNICEF, 7-10-1990.

S.K. Sharma, Director, STI(P), AIR, New Delhi, 8-1-90, *Lecture*.

Sunil Mishra, Director, Audience Research, AIR, New Delhi, 23-1-90, *Lecture*.

Other References

Dr. Premlata Sharma, Vice-Chancellor, Indira Kala Sangeet Vishvavidhlaya Khairagarh, 21-3-1988, 9.30 p.m. National Prog. of Talks, AIR, New Delhi.

H.K.L. Bhagat, Then, Minister of I&B, Govt. of India, Inaugural Speech 18-3-1988, Published in Daily M.P. Chronicle 19-3-88.

Pt. Ravishanker, TV Prog. 'Khayal', Telecast on 8-5-90.

48 Students of Various Music Colleges/Schools, Interviewed.

Index

Radio House, Apollo Bunder, Bombay

Photograph from Special Issue of Akashvani (July 24-30, 1977) published on 42nd year of publication.

Frontispiece - Marconi House London, Showing the B.B.C.'s first station, '2LO' (1922-25)

Photograph from *Broadcasting in Britain*, Keith Geddes, 1972, Her Majesty's Stationery Office, London, p. 4.

Sir J.C.W. Reith
The Founder of the Broadcasting Institution

Photograph from *The Birth of Broadcasting*, Asa Briggs

AKASHVANI

Hark to Akashvani up-surging
From here below.
The earth is bathed in Heaven's glory,
Its purple glow.
Across the blue expanse is firmly planted
The altar of the Muse ;
The lyre unheard of Light is throbbing
With human hues.
From earth to heaven, distance conquered,
In waves of light
Flows the music of man's divining,
Fancy's flight.
To East and West speech careers,
Swift as the Sun,
The mind of man reaches Heaven's confines,
Its freedom won.

(*Poem specially written for All India Radio in 1938 by Poet Tagore*)

ধরার আঙিনা হতে ঐ শোনো
উঠিল আকাশবাণী।
অমরলোকের মহিমা দিল যে
মর্ত্যলোকেরে আনি।
সরস্বতীর আসন পাতিল
নীল গগনের মাঝে,
আলোক-বীণার সভামণ্ডলে
মানুষের বীণা বাজে।
সুরের প্রবাহ ধায় সুরলোকে
দূরকে সে নেয় জিনি।
কবি-কল্পনা বহিয়া চলিল
অলখ সৌদামিনী।
ভাষা-রথ ধায় পূরবে পশ্চিমে
সূর্যরথের সাথে,
উধাও হইল মানবচিত্ত
স্বর্গের সীমানাতে॥

শান্তিনিকেতন
৫ অগস্ট
১৯৩৮

রবীন্দ্রনাথ ঠাকুর

A rare, old photograph of Rabindranath Tagore from the collection of All India Radio Calcutta and a poem specially written by him for All India Radio in 1938 with its English version

Photograph and poem from special Issue of Akashwani (July 24-30, 1977) published on 42nd year of publication.